Hadley

Finding God In Autism

Second Edition

Mary Ann Payne, M.A.

No part of this publication may be reproduced, stored in a retrieval system or transmitted in any way by any means, electronic, mechanical, photocopy, recording or otherwise without the prior permission of the author except as provided by USA copyright law.

Scripture quotations are taken from the Holy Bible, New Living Translation, copyright ©1996. Used by permission of Tyndale House Publishers, Inc., Wheaton, Illinois 60189. All rights reserved.

The opinions expressed are those of the author. This book is designed to provide accurate and authoritative information with regard to the subject matter covered. This information is given with the understanding that the author is not engaged in rendering legal, professional advice. Since the details of your situation are fact dependent, you should additionally seek the services of a competent professional.

Hadley–Second Edition
Copyright ©2017 by Mary Ann Payne, M.A.
All rights reserved.

Cover and back cover artwork by Hadley Payne

Printed by CreateSpace
www.createspace.com/7379858
Available from Amazon.com, CreateSpace.com, and other retail outlets
ISBN-10: 1973831643
ISBN-13: 978-1973831648

I was a pastor to the family for many years. I witnessed first hand how their love for one another and for God impacted Hadley's life as she grew into a beautiful young woman filled with the joy of the Lord. Hadley, in turn, has made an impact on the lives of so many others in amazing ways. Her story is one of hope, promise, and a future.
                              Rev. James H. Carlson, D. Min.

The story of Hadley, as told by her mother, is an easy-to-read, straightforward, and powerful narrative of a mother and her family confronted with the realities of raising a child with special needs. Empathy and understanding are important skills for volunteers and helping professionals alike. This book is sure to promote it.
                              Scott Sanders, PhD., Professor/Program Director/Social Work, Cornerstone University.

When passing through the valley of tears, Psalm 84:6 encourages us to make it a place of springs. Mary Ann's story of her journey with Hadley from the "why me, Lord" questions to "how can you use this, Lord?" is an inspiring example of the Psalm 84 journey possible to each of us in our personal valley of tears.
                              Judy Mohan, former editor and writer, Chicago Tribune.

"Hadley" is a heart-warming and, at times, harrowing story of one family's journey in the world of autism. You will feel the Paynes' joys and sorrows as they navigate the treacherous road of raising Hadley. You just never know what Hadley will do next! Mary Ann's stories of family, faith and friendship will lift your spirits and challenge your heart and mind. These stories are told with the intuition and love that only a mother could have, and when you've finished the book, you'll be hungry for more. Fortunately, Hadley's story is not a work of fiction, but an ongoing adventure, and I look forward to hearing more from the hectic, and often hilarious world of "Hadley."

Dr. Chris Jarrett, Keystone Church

Contents

Dedication i
Acknowledgments iii
Foreword v
Preface vii
Just the Two of Us 1
The Birth 17
A Day in a Life 23
The Move 32
The Beach 46
Sideliners 55
Holidays 62
Our Little Runaway 86
The Church 106
The School 117
The Office Visit 131
The Facts 151
The Healing 161
Afterword 205
Bibliography 209
Author contact information 211

Dedication

For our precious Hadley, an absolute angel of God.

Acknowledgments

My darling Bill, thirty years ago, who would have fathomed the precarious road predetermined for us? You have been a sturdy, invaluable partner travelling the unsettled ground. I love you my immeasurable friend.

Dearest Lauren, Jack, Alan, and Hadley, four marvelous treasures unearthed to make this world a brighter, kinder place. You are each unique in your own tender skin. My heart is contented.

Most importantly, My Lord and savior, you have held me up with your right hand. You have given me strength, support and provision while navigating this fallen world. You have restored my joy and put a new song in my heart.

My appreciations to Chris and Jen Jarrett in voluntarily reading and proofing my story, Jonathon Bosley providing technical support, and Brandon Martinez furnishing the author cover photo, all of their tireless efforts were necessary in making this manuscript happen.

Foreword

This is a collection of stories that I have written over the years regarding our daughter and her autism. Using education, inspiration, and lots of humor you will see how we were able to turn our trials into triumphs.

I have a master of arts in counseling and personnel and have worked as a case manager for over fifteen years. This is my first attempt at publication, though I have been in the process of penning the manuscript for the past eighteen years. This collection of short stories tells of fortunate and not-so-fortunate events that actually took place.

It is my intention for the reader to learn from our pain as well as our pleasure of living and dealing with autism. None of us plan on having adverse circumstances in our lives. Our circumstances can be out of our control, but it is how we react and respond accordingly that helps shape our lives. We all have a story to tell based on our life experiences and I think it is fitting to share them to teach and help one another. Using my circumstances in this story, I have made myself vulnerable in order to bless people and point them to God. I tell my story for His glory.

Upon the release of my first addition of this story in 2013 the statistics from the Centers for Disease Control announced that there were one in eighty-eight individuals on the autism spectrum. Before the ink was even dried within the year of my publication those statistics rose to *one in sixty-eight*. This is a pandemic and the *experts* can't seem to tell us the cause or the treatment. I ask God to wrestle with those who know the truth behind this alarming mystery and to push them forward to tell it.

Preface

I wrote this book for three reasons:

First, I want to give society a view into an everyday account of living with an autistic individual. This is my brutally honest contribution to autism awareness.

Second, I want to give a peek into the controversial biomedical treatment protocol that improved the quality of Hadley's life.

What works for some people may not work for others. We chose to apply alternative treatment methods for our daughter. I am not medically certified to give or suggest any advice regarding the treatment of autism. I am just sharing what worked well for our daughter.

Third and foremost, I want to show how we were able to begin a personal relationship with God and worship him in the midst of our despair.

Preface

I wrote this book for three reasons:

First, I want to give society a view into an everyday account of living with an autistic individual. This is my brutally honest contribution to autism awareness.

Second, I want to give a peek into the controversial biomedical treatment protocol that improved the quality of Hadley's life.

What works for some people may not work for others. We chose to apply alternative treatment methods for our daughter. I am not medically certified to give or suggest any advice regarding the treatment of autism. I am just sharing what worked well for our daughter.

Third and foremost, I want to show how we were able to begin a personal relationship with God and worship him in the midst of our despair.

Just the Two of Us

In the beginning God created the heavens and the earth.
Genesis 1:1

The decade was prosperous, a great beginning for two mid-western, middle-class, college-educated kids. The 1980s were flourishing and affluent. It was a great era to have graduated from college with a marketable degree. The exceedingly and abundantly economic opportunities had no boundaries. The sky was the limit. Everyone we knew was employed and doing well. It was refreshing to look forward to a new decade and leave the high inflation and depressed economy of the 1970s far behind. This would be the start of Reaganomics, the "trickle down" effects. It was new and exciting, innovative and working. Careers and entrepreneurism soared like never before. It was working well for us.

Bill, an engineer and sales representative, had established himself in a partnership. His work allowed interesting endeavors as he found himself travelling all around the world. It was not unusual for him to frequent two different continents in one week.

"Oh, Mary, you really should have been with me this time. The eatery that Joe and I were having lunch in to settle the acquisition was over four hundred years old. Darn if those folks weren't short back then. I hit my head three times entering the incredibly low doorways," Bill chuckled as he handed me a sample menu from the ancient pub.

"Did you happen to pick up my jackets from the cleaners? Remember, I leave for France on Tuesday for the start-up of the new bagging line. I sure wish that you would consider taking the time off to come with me. It would be quite romantic," his puppy-dog eyes pleaded as he pulled me close.

"Think of it, just the two of us, alone walking the streets of Paris," he said as he lovingly kissed me.

Oh, those were fast, furious, and uncultivated times.

As for me, with a master of arts in counseling and personnel, I managed to work my way up to an administrative position for social services in a thriving metropolitan area. I had been a social worker for only six years and was now enjoying the status of department head, enjoying fancy luncheons and implementing impressive programs.

"Hi, Mavis," I said on the phone while in my Lexus agency car. "I am only about an hour now from the office. Could you please have those discharge papers on Mrs.

Smith ready for me to sign? Oh, and, Mavis, could you have my French vanilla latte on my desk for me when I get there?"

"Oh, Mavis, it's raining cats and dogs out here!"

"What's that, Mavis? No, I didn't finish it yet. Tell the community block grant writer that I will need one more week to finalize the report for the women's shelter. Thanks so much, Mavis. You really make it all happen for me. I love you Mavis. See you in twenty minutes."

I call all the shots; I prided myself—no more trenches for me!

We had arrived. Bill and I had really made it. The American dream had unfolded before our eyes. We were now nestled in "Scarsdale"—a swanky, upbeat, high-end neighborhood in a suburban community. Our combined income had afforded us everything. Want was a thing of the past. We used airliners as though they were taxis. Among our peers, it became snobbishly cool to outwit the others in describing an unusual culinary experience that we may have had.

"Yes, that's right, Sal. Last night while dinning at Chez Antoine's we had the most amazing *foie gras*, followed by *salad nicoise*, topped with poached quail egg—just to die for," I bragged while standing around the water cooler.

Us yuppies were in full force. We were in control. The world was ours. We not only had two incomes; we had monumental incomes. We glided about in leather-lined, luxurious Lexus, Beamers, and Infinities. This was the generation of "big boy" toys like no other generation before. We were the first ones on our block to sport a mobile cellular phone. (The phones at that time actually had to be installed into your vehicle!) We used to love to pick up our friends and, while on the way to dinner, with an intentional nonchalance, casually pick up the mobile phone and call to check on our reservation, just because we could. Our toys were incredibly high-tech and we loved them. We were on top of the wave. "What more could we possibly want?" we asked.

Children!

As life would have it, the years moved on and the demands at the office continued to increase. The toys and stuff, though all very fascinating, just didn't completely satisfy us anymore. So we did what all-good yuppie Americans do—we had children. The children seemed to arrive with little to no discussion at all. It just seemed to be the next natural order of business for us. The children soon occupied our home and commanded our time. It was wonderful even though our world was no longer our own. The "two of us" morphed into the "four of us." We would begin our own personal bit of history. We would start our own nucleus of a family. Our lives would never be the same and would begin to change drastically. But weren't we doing our duty? After all, hadn't the Lord commanded that we procreate and populate the earth? It was only fair that we do our part.

Hence the children came and our lives began changing along with our needs. We began to sell off our beloved toys. We needed to prioritize some things—maybe even trade some stuff for other stuff. Sailboats and home-recording studios just didn't seem as important anymore when you didn't have time for them anyway. We needed a bigger house. We needed a bigger yard to accommodate the other two people. Beamers were traded in for minivans. Tennis rackets were removed from car trunks in exchange for diaper bags. We found ourselves immersed in Disney animated movies for the next decade instead of viewing the latest popular sitcoms. Colleagues ten years our junior would be roaring at the break table over last evening's episode of *Friends* while we turned a deaf ear and began humming happily to the tune of "Some Day My Prince Will Come." Oh, how the tides had turned. Big things seemed so little and little things seemed so big. Someone had once said to me, "Different ages, different stages." We were definitely entering a different stage in our lives.

Yet still at the top of the wave, we had double income with two kids. We were living in one of the most exciting cities in the world. We had amazing and wonderful jobs and careers. We were also privileged with the best restaurants and shopping that the big city could offer. The cultural events were immense and endless. We could scarcely take it all in. Our lives were huge! Friday nights seemed to knock at the door of Monday mornings. Time sped by at the speed of light.

We were also regular attendees of a very progressive mega church because somewhere deep down, buried in our busy hearts, we knew that God existed, but we just didn't have much time for him, "We will catch you later God," we said to our selves. Yet we happily and ritually attended the services, as any proper all-American Christian family should do. All was good.

Though we mostly ignored God in our day-to-day life, we thanked him for all of the blessings bestowed upon us. We were enjoying all of the rewards and pleasures that the world could offer. We ignored the thought that we were becoming distracted from the more important things in life. And we knew that deep down, somewhere in our hearts, we were becoming more devoted to the world than we were to God.

Thus, we continued on the treadmill of life. The usual office demands, the mundane household chores, the perfunctory family and neighborhood socials, and of course the weekly church attendance rolled on and on. Life was so good. What could possibly go wrong?

As fate would have it, our wave crashed down upon us. Our world was in perfect order, or so we thought until that cold afternoon in 1994.

The kids were laughing and playing and running all over the room. It was closing time here at the "Love Me Do Day Care." You could hear giggles and sobs and "Yes, I cans" and "No, you cants" and "My dog is bigger than yours." You could see scrapes, runny noses, and untied shoes. It was complete pandemonium. It was mayhem. It was normal children at play. It was wonderful. It was where our children had taken up residency during the week for the past five years. It was the official site for all the children of very-busy-working mommies and daddies. This was the familiar scene we would encounter each night as we hurried from our busy offices to snatch up our most important commodities. Each weeknight at 5:45 p.m. sharp, like robots, we, double-income, harried parents, filed in through the doors of employed strangers to whom we daily entrusted our children.

I walked deep into the jungle, carefully stepping over makeshift tents and make-believe rivers and lakes. I diligently tiptoed over and under the games and play-acting of highly active and enthusiastic children. I had to make sure I did not crush any creative imaginary boundaries.

Maybe today, I pondered, as I continued to carefully maneuver my way through the mirage of merriment. Maybe today would be different, I sighed. Please, God! I secretly prayed. But my eyes brimmed over with tears as that invisible hammer took another swing at my heart. What I saw had been no different from the past few months at the end of the day when it was time to pick up my children and go home.

Why, Lord? Why wasn't she playing with anyone? Why was she just sitting there, staring blankly into space as if no one else was in the room? As if she couldn't see all the spontaneous frolicking around her. Why couldn't she hear the pleading for her to join in the fun from her peers? Could my baby be deaf? I wondered.

Hadley, at the age of three, sat silent, mute, unattached, and lifeless at the day care center. The beautiful little girl just sat there in the midst of all her surroundings as if she were on another planet a million miles away.

Is there anyone out there who can help me? I cried at

this troubling sight. There was something terribly wrong with my child, and no one seemed to want to help me! Is there not one person who can help me? I lamented.

Each night that I came to pick up my baby, the caregivers, barely able to look me in the eyes, would recite the same dismal report of Hadley's detachment from her peers and environment. I silently grieved on those long, sad nightly drives back to our home from the day care.

Within the first year, we noticed Hadley being different; we had been to every psychologist, psychiatrist, speech therapist, neurologist, social worker, and social scientist listed in the American Medical Association. But no one seemed to know what to do about Hadley. In fact, at the time, nobody was even in agreement as to what to call it— this thing that seemed to have robbed me of my baby. No one had any answers. However, they all had the same old conclusion that nothing would ever change for her.

"Have you heard about that new treatment approach called audio training?" the school social worker asked one afternoon as I picked Hadley up from preschool.

"Why no, I haven't," I said. "What do you know about it, Sherry?"

I explained everything that Sherry had told me in detail to Bill as we drove the hour-and-a-half route each way to yet another possible hopeful solution for Hadley.

"Maybe this treatment will be 'the cure,'" I cried desperately to Bill as he patiently drove on.

But unfortunately for us, after ten sessions in a row, at one hundred dollars a pop (that was not covered by our insurance), this again had proved not to be the cure. Poor

Hadley had to endure those long; arduous drives while struggling to sit buckled in her seat. Then she had to sit again for a half hour donning heavy-weighted earphones in order to supposedly have some sort of high frequency pitch connect within her inner ear that would improve her disability in some way. Nothing had changed after these treatments and Hadley was still the same. Yes, we were desperate and willing to try just about anything that sounded like it might be of benefit for our daughter. Bill and I were willing to crawl to the ends of the earth if that was what it would take to find a cure for our daughter.

Hadley would always be different the professionals would continue to claim.

"You will need to learn to deal with her just as she is," they told me. But I just could not, or stubbornly would not, accept this. I didn't want to deal with her as she was. I wanted my perfect baby back! I grew tired and depressed in my desperate search for help with no real answers or solutions to work with. Even though I tried to find solutions on my own, I was getting nowhere fast. Hadley was still the same, simply there but not there.

As a believer, I had been told all my life that good things come from God. God did not make bad things. God does not make mistakes. After all, he had created the heavens and the earth. Certainly he wouldn't have created a child like this, I reasoned. I somehow was convinced that he did not create this, whatever it was, this problem with Hadley. I truly believed with all my heart and soul that God did not have a direct hand in it. I believed that he did not make this happen to my daughter as some had tried to convince me. Whatever this thing was that seemed to have happened to her was allowed to happen but not intended or designed by God. My ears burned as I remembered just three years earlier, at her birth, the doctor's gleeful word "Perfect!"

"God, please help me find the answers," I begged. "Put the right people in my path to show me what to do. God, I know that you are there. Though I confess that I have pushed you out of my life, I desperately need you now! If you really exist then please make your self real to me."

At the end of every tunnel there is a light, but first you must be willing to navigate the darkness. The next three years are what I call the dark years. The "asylum" would be an accurate way to describe our home. We knew that something was not right with our Hadley but couldn't quite put our finger on it. No one else could either. It isn't normal when your child seems to be in constant distress. It isn't normal when your child stops talking and refuses to make eye contact. It is very abnormal when your child walks on her toes and flaps her arms as though they were the wings of a bird.

We groped in the dark on a day-to-day basis, just trying to survive one day at a time. The rest of the world moved in a usual, normal fashion, but not us. I wanted them to stop and take notice, but they just kept right on marching without us. We were on the start of the journey of living on the other side of life—the other life that does not offer mommy-daughter hugs and kisses or the life that offers nights of curling hair and baking cookies. No warm and fuzzy mellow moments with my little girl. Instead it was more like a constant fight with a complete stranger to complete the most nominal tasks. Night after tiresome night of what should be simple routines of bathing, hair brushing, and dressing became battles beyond my control. Mere, simple, ordinary household chores became excruciatingly indescribable and arduous. There seemed to be a constant shrill ringing through the house—a shrill that was coming from a little girl's mouth that should instead have been humming and singing sweet songs. With speech completely gone now, Hadley would only point, grunt, or scream at the top of her lungs. She appeared to be in some sort of constant physical pain. She did not want to be near us or be held. She spent most of her time in what appeared to be her own world.

These characteristics were normal coming from an autistic child, according to the medical and school experts who uttered the "A" word to us for the first time.

"There is not much more that you can expect from her. We believe that she has autism, and we don't really know much about treatment at this time," they would proclaim.

"So you mean to tell me that for the next ten years or more I will be getting a complete aerobic workout while merely trying to dress my little girl? You mean to tell me that for the next ten years or so my shins will be black and blue from her kicking and bucking while I give her a nightly bath? You're basically saying to me, 'Get used to the nonstop, random for-no-apparent-reason high-pitch screaming for the rest of *my life*?'" I cried.

"Keep her comfortable, safe, and dry," replied the "experts" with feigned authority.

I wanted the whole world to stop and realize what this horrible thing had done to our child and our family. I wanted them to know that this was not supposed to have happened to the two of us! But they wouldn't, and I found myself becoming bitter and angry.

Friends frequented our home less and less as we battled this mysterious autism. They didn't want their children to come over to play, nor did they invite us into their homes, afraid that their kids might "catch this thing"—this thing, whatever it was. This thing that was not normal! Were people really afraid of my child? I gasped!

We too were afraid of what others were beginning to say about us. Not only were our friends afraid of our child, but they also were slowly becoming wary of us. We were no longer that sharp, well dressed, "stylin'" couple. We were instead sporting bloodshot eyes and puffy faces that hinted of lack of sleep. We were afraid that our friends would no longer be interested in us since even we could feel the life and light dimming from our eyes.

"No, Bill, I didn't get anyone to babysit for Saturday night."

"We haven't been out with anyone for months," Bill protested.

"I am sorry that we cannot go to the club with the gang, but no one will come here anymore to sit with the kids. I swear, the last girl we had told everyone in the neighborhood about the horrors of the 'House of Payne.'"

And quite truthfully I didn't blame any of them. I knew what it was like to be around this calamity of a child.

Those fears pulled us farther and farther from life, and

we felt ourselves sinking to the bottom of the ocean.

So much for the top of the wave, it had crested and was coming down with a mighty, forceful crash. It took me down, far down to the deep end of the dark bottom. There I stayed for two years.

It is amazing how the human body can perform perfunctorily while immersed in a depressed fog. Things still needed to get done. They just don't get done very well. My life was changing and heading down a path that I did not plan for. I started gaining weight because I had stopped running my usual three miles each night. I couldn't explain my sudden weak muscle tone in my legs that precluded me from my nightly aerobic ritual. *Maybe I am just tired and depressed*, I thought. *Things will get better*, I promised myself.

But they didn't get better. In fact, they got a lot worse as time went on.

I couldn't go on like this. It was all too much now trying to keep a brave face at the office and pretending that everything was fine at home.

It must have been by the grace of God that I finally decided to come up for air. I was tired of feeling sorry for my unfortunate situation. It suddenly became clear to me within that year of madness that things needed to change and in a very drastic way. I needed to snap out of it, and quickly, if I was going to be of any value to my Hadley. I decided I was going to devote the rest of my life to this child. "I know what I need to do," I proclaimed. "I need to quit my job."

Without hesitation, Bill and I agreed that I would quit my job and be a stay-at-home mom. Move over, Helen Keller, Annie Sullivan's got nothing on me! If she could figure out that child of hers, certainly I could figure out mine. I traded in my briefcase for a clean new apron and readied myself for the next chapter of my life— motherhood. I was finally at home for the first time in our married life, full-time. This gave me all the time in the world to get reacquainted with my baby. There would be no more nannies, housekeepers, or day care centers for us.

While at home, it didn't take me long to discover that if I took my eyes off Hadley even for a split second, we could find ourselves in the midst of the biggest crisis one could imagine. For example, there was the evening when I was peeling potatoes at the kitchen sink. I walked the few feet down the corridor and glanced in on the family room to check on Hadley. There she was all smiles and playing. She seemed to be amused looking at the stripes on the sofa. A thought of elation came over me. Could this be a sign of improvement? Yes, that's it. She wanted to try to count the stripes on the sofa. Hadn't I tried numerous times to engage her in such an activity? It was finally kicking in. All that tedious work was finally paying off.

"Number one comes first. That's right, baby girl," I gently instructed. "Number two, three, and four," and so on I repeated. She was finally getting it! We were good here. All was well, nothing to worry about. I confidently skipped back to the kitchen to attend to my potatoes. I thought I'd go ahead and just peel the whole bag and then go back and check on Hadley. After all, not only was she amused and contented, but my baby could count! "She is a little genius!" I proclaimed.

Ten minutes later, as the last peel was going down the sink, I heard a noise louder than the garbage disposal.

"*Mary!*" the voice cried.

My knees buckled out from under me at the vibrant wail. With much trepidation, I found my way once more down the hall to answer the call. Bill had just come in the front door from work. He just stood there, too shocked to speak. He just stood there with his mouth hanging down to his chin. It took me a couple of seconds to fix my gaze from Bill to Hadley. Then as I saw it, and I shook with horror! There it was, our eight-foot-long, brand-new sofa smeared with human feces from top to bottom. Hadley didn't miss a spot! Her artistic ability allowed her to completely cover every inch.

Oh, Lord! Where do I begin? What will I... How will I...

As I stood there perplexed and mortified, I couldn't help but notice the satisfied look on her face. It was the look of what perhaps Rembrandt himself must have had on his face after completing one of his great masterpieces.

During those years of uncertainty, I couldn't get through one day without clinging to the word of God. I often asked myself how people did it without him. For me, from now on, it would be utterly impossible. He supplied a peace that surpassed all understanding each and every time that I cleaned up yet one more exasperating mess. That peace afforded me the ability to endure the madness I was suffering.

I realized that I needed God with me at all times, not just on Sundays! I had to literally live by one of my favorite proverbs: "Trust in the Lord with all your heart and lean not on your own understanding; in all your ways acknowledge Him, and He will make your paths straight." (Proverbs 3:5–6) And trust me, I was walking sideways! Besides, where else could I go? Man had already struck (I will explain later) and turned me away, leaving me for the most part to cope on my own.

Though we were beginning to trust, we were still taking baby steps, and it would be a long while before we would learn to completely turn everything over to God.

The Birth

What more could we possibly want? I had asked when it was just the two of us. "*Children!*" we cried with elation.

Looking back, it was the most spectacular October morning ever. I don't remember when the fall colors showed themselves so brilliantly. The trees were ablaze with burnt orange, deep russet, and golden yellow. The succulent scent of autumn was intense and intoxicating. Everywhere I looked, the amazing seasonal backdrop appeared as an illustrious treat that engulfed my senses. It was truly the paintbrush in the hand of the Almighty.

The temperature was lower than normal. The sun came in through my window and gently woke me. As I gained morning consciousness, I felt that familiar twinge in my belly and my loins known only by a mother. That twinge of a baby that was coming and wanting out fast! No one being able to deny my maternal instincts, I made the phone call to the office. I would not be having lunch with the girls today.

"Yes, Mavis, you need to call in my replacement temp.

Yes, that's right, Mavis. No, I won't be coming in. I am quite sure that today's the day. Feel free to call me in a few days if you need me for anything."

I felt powerful! This was not my first rodeo. I was a pro now, having travelled this rite of passage of "true womanhood" once before. I didn't know much about old Scarlet, but I did know something about birthing babies! I was prepared. I was confident and ready to take charge of my destiny. I knew the hour had come. And yet, being the expert that I deemed myself, I saw no need to panic. What was the hurry? After all, just two years prior, I had spent twenty-seven arduous hours in labor, waiting for that first bundle of joy. We had plenty of time. Time was on my side.

Lounging on the sofa during my second round of "aah-hee, aah-haas," the latest, state-of-the-art in birthing exercises, I started to get dizzy, but it wasn't because of my breathing exercises. I was dizzy because Bill was sprinting around our living room so fast that my head was spinning. He was ready to go and at record speed. He apparently forgot about the many rounds of crazy eights we had played to pass the twenty-seven hours during our first birthing experience with Jack. He was ready to go. I was not sure, but at first glance, I thought I saw Bill, in all his confusion, snatch the two-year-old and toss him in the dog's cage while grabbing the dog and handing her off to the sitter.

The perplexed sitter politely gulped, patted Bill on the back, and made the proper adjustments.

"Whoa, Nellie! What's the rush?" I asked. "I only have

four nails polished with six more to go."

"Hurry up and go, Mommy," little Jack pleaded. "Julie promised to build an entire Lego kingdom with me with castles and even a moat."

Julie gave me a reassuring nod as if to say, "We'll be fine. Go on; get going, as she waved her hand toward the door.

As Bill came running down the stairs he shouted, "I just spoke with your doctor who insists that with labor pains two minutes apart, the time to get to the hospital is now!" Bill instructed.

Seeing the urgency in Bill's eyes, I decided not to argue and boarded the van with the pre-packed suitcase. Expertly navigating the traffic, Bill drove me to the hospital and had me in the elevator heading to the maternity ward in what seemed like the blink of an eye. A young couple squeezed over to let us in. A brave new mom, on her way to her first breathing class, offered a lively, "First time for me."

In which I proudly boasted, "Second one for me!"

With my chest puffed out as far as my belly, the scream that escaped me echoed loudly off the four walls of the packed elevator. I didn't even realize that the sound left my mouth! That labor pain crept up on me fast and caught me by surprise. Feeling like I was no longer in control, I knew that I had run out of time.

As the elevator doors finally opened, I turned to give my new friend a quick "good luck" only to discover that she had fainted into the arms of her husband. What happened next seemed to take place in a nanosecond.

I was snatched off the elevator and was thrown onto a

gurney while being pushed rapidly by someone that I could not see. Expertly rounding the corners, a nurse, doing her best to keep up the pace of the fast-moving gurney, appeared out of nowhere.

She pulled back my blanket and cried, "Lord, have mercy! Head for delivery, this baby is really coming"

An orderly threw some surgical scrubs two sizes too small at Bill and shoved him down a long hallway with many doors. He told him to go change and hurry. The look on Bill's confused face said, "Which door?" I was sure I would never see him again that day.

It was now time for lights, camera, and action! So much for the deck of cards I had packed. There would be no rounds of crazy eights this time.

All the while I kept wondering where my doctor was. I had completely given up on Bill. Why was it that each time I was having a baby there was never a doctor in the house? I can only speak from my own experience, regarding birth, as mine were predominately orchestrated by nurses on staff and not by doctors at all. In both of my experiences, my doctor was in the middle of an important tennis match. Of course each time I was told not to worry, as they were only a phone call away. I am convinced that there must be a secret room set aside in hospital wings throughout America where nurses can award each other with trophies for completion of successful birthing procedures.

The girls were brilliant! It was all like some slow motion, well-rehearsed medical symphony. First, there was a nurse behind me who was gently stroking my hair. Second, there was a nurse at the foot of my bed who was expertly adjusting my legs into the stir-ups. A third nurse, with great precision and little effort, injected IVs and applied blood pressure cuffs. A fourth, ever so motherly, served thin, fresh ice chips to the Sahara Desert in my mouth.

Aside from the mounting pain, I could have stayed there all my life. What pampering. I felt like a true lady in waiting. Who would want to go home? The patting of the forehead with a cool, damp cloth; the soothing and encouraging words; and the comforting massage to my feet, legs, and shoulders, all felt dreamy. What a way to take an excruciatingly painful experience and make it incredibly desirable. Still the baby was coming.

The symphonic production was coming to its climax. The nurse at the foot of my bed played the role of the conductor. She melodiously sang out orders to the pit band camouflaged as the other nurses. They sang back in perfect harmony.

"Push now!" one sang.

"Blood pressure normal," the other chimed in.

"Vital signs looking good. Head bearing down the canal."

They all sang on pitch and in perfect harmony. What music to my ears. Finally, the concert was coming to an end.

The conductor nurse proudly announced, "And now for the moment we all have been waiting for, the final movement!"

And then suddenly, out of nowhere, he appeared.

"It's show time," the elated doctor cried as he danced

into the room. Setting down his tennis racket and tossing aside the exhausted nurses, he stepped right into the center stage to conclude the performance and take his bow. Unlike the wilted nurses, he appeared to be fresh as a daisy. As though he had been there all morning, he routinely positioned his hands to couple the baby's head. At this point, I didn't care who delivered her. I just wanted to meet my baby. As he extracted her from me, allowing her to take her first breath, he skillfully examined her and jubilantly cried out, *"Perfect!"*

God designed marriage and told us to have children to populate the earth. This was one of the happiest days of our lives for Bill and I. Our little family was now complete. So we thought.

The word *perfect* would later haunt me for the rest of my life.

You made all the delicate, inner parts of my body and knit me together in my mother's womb.

Psalms 139:13

A Day in a Life

The births of our children, as for many couples, were some of the happiest moments of our lives. God had truly blessed us as we proclaimed that our family was complete. It was complete, all right—*completely* different from what we could have ever imagined in a million years. It was so different that I came up with a new concept called living on the other side of life. This concept means that when a seemingly once normal life becomes "abnormal," you now live on the other side of life. The normal limits are defined by the rest of the world, whatever that may be, and abnormal is not a part of it. This may occur when some unforeseen circumstance is laid upon you out of nowhere; of no volition of your own, it descends upon you.

In our case, it was the unfortunate diagnosis of autism for my daughter, Hadley, at the age of three. Since that dreadful day, our family found itself living on the outside looking in. We were now living on what I call the other side of life. Prior to quitting my job and becoming a stay-at-home mom, we often found ourselves in dire situations regarding the public. I guess I was so preoccupied with my work to realize that our little family really was different. It was as if, suddenly, we found ourselves being stamped with a sign on our foreheads that read: damaged goods, outcast, and second-class citizen. Then there was the face of the others reading the sign, the face that revealed the presumption of "glad it's them and not us." Or the face of the pious judge chiding, "They sure must have done something really bad to deserve that!" Or they murmur, "Stay clear, leper approaching." And on and on it goes.

The bomb was dropped, our world was now upside down, and what seemed normal for us at one time was now very abnormal. No matter whom we were with or where we would happen to go, people just looked at us differently now.

"Hey, Mommy, why do all the people stare at Hadley when we go places?

"Why do they make mean faces at my little sister? Don't they know that she can't help it?" Jack's innocence would ask.

The *Webster's Dictionary* defines the word *normal* as "one that is normal, not deviating from the norm. Relating to or characterized by average intelligence or development. Free from disorder of body and mind."[1] Well, that certainly sums it up. If you do not fit the above description, then you are not normal. Just that simple, you are different. You now must live in a very different camp because you do not fit in. It could be characterized like that of a round hole and a square peg.

Now that you are different, normal people may treat you accordingly with no uncertain terms. It is their way, it is their right, and, after all, they are normal. But it is not just the treatment of people that traps you to live on the other side of life; it is simply everyday life itself. Life is not made for the abnormal.

When you live on the other side of life, the simplest task can become monumental. The most ordinary task can be complex. You learn what are considered to be safe places and what are not. You learn who are considered to be safe people and who are not. The act of leaving your own home can become a dangerous adventure. The moment you close that door behind you and step outside, you enter a place that was basically designed for normal people, not you. You are like foreigners in a different land. Nobody speaks your language. And the natives are not exactly very friendly.

Now going in and out of your home is as normal as breathing in and out if you are normal. The outside is waiting for you. The outside is prepared to serve you. It is waiting to supply your every whim. The world is made for those who are normal. You are all the same and you all fit in. You are worthy.

Hence, the yearning is so great to be with the normal people again, as it is so appealing on the normal side of life. The abnormal occasionally try to fill the hunger, the emptiness, and the curiosity. This feeling of deprivation allows you to become brave enough to, occasionally, throw all caution to the wind. To have a sense of "enter at your own risk because here we come. I can't take it anymore. I must see how the other side lives. I must have what they have no matter what the consequences are." This being said, allow me to invite you to dinner.

It was a night similar to a normal family of two working parents with children. Rush hour had been successfully mastered. Babies with runny noses were picked up from day care. Hugs and kisses were exchanged. Mail was sorted, and the dog was let out. E-mail was checked and cleared. All that was left to do was to throw the chicken into the oven to satisfy the hunger pangs of what looked like three starved lions mimicking my husband and two children.

As I walked over to the empty sink, I started to get that sick feeling. You know the one. It's the feeling that smacks of horror. It's the feeling that turns into a voice somewhere in the back of your head. "How could you, you dummy!" it shouts. After all, you only got up at four thirty in the morning to mop the kitchen floor, write the week's grocery list, investigate the invoice of the office visit not covered, make the day's lunch for two, lay out the day's clothing for four, prepare and serve the morning's breakfast, kennel the dog, brush teeth, bathe, shower, and promptly head out into the morning's rush hour traffic! Did I mention drop babies off at the day care and make it to the office by eight? "How could you have forgotten to thaw the chicken for our dinner?" scolded the voice. I felt very flustered as the voice did its guilt-ridden job, the lions circling me.

"We're hungry, Mom. What's for dinner?" asked Jack

I had to think fast. Quick, what to do?

"We are going out for dinner," I boldly announced.

Now for the family of the abnormal, the act of going out to dinner is not an easy feat. It is labor intensive, it is trepidation, it is an adventure, and it is truly rare. As I describe the events of the evening as they unfolded, don't be surprised if they appear similar to that of a three-act play.

Act I: The Set

Upon the arrival to our neighborhood restaurant, as fate would have it, the table closest to the door was not available. For us this was not good. Being the family that we had become, we needed the table closest to the door. Things were likely to start to get abnormal for sure and we would require a quick and easy getaway. We perused the menu as we waited in the long line but eventually got seated.

Unfortunately, the table was all the way in the back of the restaurant. It had to be at least a football field's length away from the front door. For us, the distance to the front door (otherwise known as the escape hatch) was crucial. For the abnormal family, a small, overcrowded, stuffy dining room is a sure recipe for disaster. For us, strange things just start to happen—things that other normal people do not like. When those things start to happen, it is as if the room actually begins to close in on us. There is no extra space for the child who must pace. For the "special" child, it is like being a caged wild animal with no escape.

Bill and I could sense the restricted urgency to release

itself building within our child as we waited an extra long time for our food. We began to chew our *escargot* and swallowed as fast as we could. We had been in this situation before. By golly, this time we were going to make it. After all, we had only been seated for about a half an hour, and, oh, how I longed for a night out on the town. We were not only going to make it through the main course, but we were determined to see the dessert cart this night.

We continued to devour our *hors d' oeuvres* through nervous smiles and gulps as we felt rapidly darting eyes upon us. We knew the signals but kept trying to pretend, hoping this night would be different. Hadley continued to squirm as she pushed the appetizers around with her fork. For the third time her fork left her grasp and fell crashing onto her plate, breaking the mellow mood of the room. Icy glares were launched our way.

Now going for the Academy Award: Hadley's whine and whimpers grew louder and longer. The whimpers turned to outbursts. The outbursts seemed to stretch her vocal chords clear up to the ceiling. For what seemed like no apparent reason, this child was monstrously out of control. She had reached all of her limits. She was clutching her blanket while yelping and screeching as if being tortured. This obnoxious obtrusion sliced right through the peaceful ambiance of the room of the casual diners. They were not happy and rightfully so.

Act II: The Climax

The event was in full bloom. Our hopes had been

shattered again. For us there would be no main course, no dessert cart tonight after all. *Why couldn't we just go out for a simple dinner?* I despaired. I suddenly felt myself sinking back to the bottom of the ocean. I just wanted to fade away into the woodwork. That's when the angry shrill jolted me.

"Lady!" the voice sneered.

My sad eyes refocused upon the annoyed waiter. I was slowly resurfacing from the bottom of the ocean when the second jolt of his voice abruptly brought me back.

"The first thing you need to do is get rid of that blanket!" he shouted. I felt the blow to my heart. *Don't take it to heart, don't listen to the words*, I consoled myself. *And whatever you do, just nod in compliance.*

"The second thing you need to do..." Yes, he was really on number two. Remember, this was a live event, with real audience and spectators.

The spectators were on his side; after all, they were all normal and it was their right. Go, brother, their concurring heads nodded. They could see that we were in tow with a "special" child by now, but how dare we ruin their night? If only they had known, as well as us, what we would learn many years later. Hadley's immune system had somehow been compromised, which caused gastrointestinal discomfort. Unbeknown to us at the time, this caused her to experience extreme physical pain simply by eating foods that contained gluten and casein (proteins in wheat and dairy found to be indigestible for some people).

Had we just known that much information at the time, the agony and extreme pain we could have spared her, not to mention the other diners in the restaurant! We might even have had a chance to actually finish a meal while dining out. All those years, I thought in hindsight, of motherly buttering her bread, not knowing that she simply couldn't digest it, causing my baby horrific pain.

Act III: The Curtain

"What you really ought to do is give her a good spanking," he ranted.

I swallowed my last bite of escargot for the evening, along with my pride. Within seconds, I was expertly able to pick up our obtrusive entourage. With eyes averted, we made our way to the beloved door. As Bill held open the door, my soon-to-be escape to sanctuary, and I with one leg out of it, I turned back. I locked eyes with the unyielding, outspoken, uninformed waiter and said, "I ought to spank you."

Curtain down, the end…

"Lord, you said, 'Be angry, but do not sin' (Ephesians 4:26). Please help me not to sin."

Too late again, I thought. If only I could accept this fate and handle things better. If only I could have apologized to the diners and maybe offered some educational information on the ill behaviors of autism.

This is just one example of how I had to learn to live in obedience to God's Word on a daily basis now that we were living with autism. I had to learn how to apply his Word in every area of my life. Most times it seemed I was failing miserably. In the very early years of dealing with autism, we had some pretty harsh encounters and situations with people. Looking back, I know that they just didn't understand it anymore than we did ourselves.

A day in a life was far more than I could bear at times. *Dear God if you are there will you help me?* It would be years later before I could start to feel his peace and begin to acknowledge my burden being lifted. *I must learn to trust in him and move forward with boldness*, I humbly thought.

"Could you be my only hope? Lord, please help me to focus on you during these tough trials."

I love the Lord because he hears my voice and my prayer for mercy.

Psalms 116:1

The Move

Feeling as though I had exhausted all of the resources in the radius of my immediate world in order to help my daughter, it was time to move on. There had to be more out there somewhere to give me help to improve the quality of her life. It was time to go.

The city that I had loved was now my nemesis. It rejected my daughter and it rejected us. In no uncertain terms, it was clear that we didn't fit in. Nothing made sense anymore. There were so many people everywhere but no one seemed to have a face. And when they did, it wasn't a friendly one. What once was the great, vast enamor of cultural festivities and culinary confections that a big city has to offer, was now morphing right before my eyes. Nothing it had to offer could any longer lend itself to us. I could almost see the tall buildings bending over, sprouting arms to strangle us. "Get out! Move on!" they cried.

I began to see things differently. There was an endless

trail of traffic spewing exhaust, choking and clouding my vision. What was once exhilarating, rich, and inspiring now seemed frightening, empty, and hollow. It was no longer a place for us in which to raise a child, and certainly not a special child.

My once beloved big city, the place of social and cultural surroundings that helped shape our lives, now subjected me to feelings of despair. The feelings were so strong that I felt a need to literally sew Hadley right to my hip so as not to lose her in the crowd. Any place we went outside of our home was considered enemy ground. No place was safe. A simple jaunt to the grocery store was a nightmare. I knew no one. I trusted no one. Everyone in the store could be suspect to foul play should Hadley break free from my grasp.

I had to shelter this helpless, unsuspecting child. I had to protect her from harm. With no available family near us, no real close friends, we basically had no help, period. Though we attended a church at the time, we chose not to participate in terms of small group activities. We attended the church but did not become involved with anyone. We kept to ourselves. That was a huge mistake on our part that we would not discover until later. What seemed like total isolation from people became the final straw. That was the breaking point. Hadley was now four years old and we could no longer stay here in the city. But where would we go? We needed help, we needed people, and we needed answers.

Bill and I were the last two people on the planet to make rash decisions. As a matter of fact, we were known as the people who would research things to death. For example, if one of our friends were planning to purchase a car, they would call us first to consult because they knew we would have all the current statistics and information readily available. We would know which vehicles offered the best gas mileage, the best safety ratings and the best resale value. They could count on us. The work was already done for them. As with all decisions, it was our nature to weigh things down to the last ounce. We would analyze things up one side and down the other.

So it was no wonder that when we suddenly quit our jobs, sold our beloved home, packed up the kids, and left town, all our friends thought that we had taken complete leave of our senses.

Not just them; even we questioned our own sanity. I often wondered if this was what Abraham, felt like when he was told to go and seek out a foreign land (Genesis 12:1). He didn't know where he was going. He didn't ask where. He just went. He believed and trusted. At this point in my life, I needed that kind of faith.

Like Abraham of ancient times, we too felt as though we were being sent on a journey—not knowing why but just having an urgency to go. We left all that was familiar to us and headed out for a new frontier. Later it would become clear to us that this journey was about much more than just our daughter.

During these dark years in our lives, we began to pray a lot. We questioned God. We wondered why this autism thing had happened to Hadley. Didn't we already believe in Him? Was all this necessary to get our attention? The people asked in ancient times, "Lord, which of the parents sinned to have had this affliction upon them?" (John 9:3). Trust me, we both felt guilty. We couldn't help but blame ourselves for something we did or didn't do. We also wondered about what had actually happened to Hadley. She was absolutely healthy and normal one minute and gone from us the next. The pediatrician pronounced month after month that she was meeting all her milestones for a normal baby. Yet it was as if an alien had come in the middle of the night around the age of three. This alien stole her away and replaced her with someone who looked like Hadley but the life had vanished from her eyes.

During those years, she appeared to be in constant physical pain and inconsolable distress. No one would give me answers to my questions or suggestions to help us. I just wanted to run away. It was during those days that I could almost hear God saying, "Believe in me, trust in me, and go for I have a very special place for you."

So just as the ancient prophet before us, we set off to the wilderness. Not knowing what to expect. Not knowing what lay ahead. We just knew we had to make our world a bit smaller and safer enough to better manage Hadley. If the Lord is directing your path, then why worry about the steps along the way (Proverbs: 20:24)?

So were we, in fact, crazy like our friends implied, or were we just simply being led? Did we just go on a whim of desperation, or did God tell us to go? We struggled with those questions for years. I want to believe the latter. Later, the latter would prove to be true. I know because we had to climb up every rung.

For years we had vacationed in a small, northern, coastal resort town in Michigan. Could this be that very special place we were being lead to? I wondered. I never dreamt in a million years that this would become our future home—that big old blue house one block from the beach.

As far as Bill was concerned that house was nothing more than a drafty old dilapidated barn. I'll never forget the day that I spotted it. It was right there across the street from the hotel that we were staying in while on vacation in that small town. It was for sale and I had finally convinced Bill to go in and take a look inside. And there we stood. There we were two adults, back to back, with our arms defiantly crossed over our chests. I looked around at the vast, 110 year old beauty and saw the great potential that I knew that she possessed.

"Possessed" is the word that Bill used to describe me as he looked around, shook his head and walked right out the door. Yes, I guess it was quite different from our lovely home back in the city. The home that was a 1940's style vintage colonial, 4,500 square feet, custom built abode with solid floors that were flat and straight.

"But Bill it's just as spacious as our other house and it even has an extra room upstairs to be made into a clubhouse for the kids," I begged.

"You know how much Hadley loves her music and CD's, I droned on. Heck, she can play her music up there at

2000 decibels if she wants and no one would even care. Besides, I like the fact that this house is a bit worn. It's not so fancy as our house back home. We won't even care about the little 'Hadley' accidents. This house would be much more forgiving," I pleaded.

Well, I don't know who was more forgiving over the years, Bill or that old house. Bill ended up buying that house for me. Then he and all of the local contractors spent the next ten years painstakingly keeping it from falling down. It seemed that it would require drilling, sawing, and hammering on everything from the roof to the kitchen sink on my gem of a house. Got to give us credit for employing half of the community.

It took about ten laborious years to finally get the place to Bill's fancy. Now, even he walks around the big old barn and admires his rebuilt accomplishment of a home.

Many a night while swaying slowly on our beloved porch swing he gets confirmation of a deed well done from passers by.

"Quite a place you folks have here."

"Sure love your flowers"

"Wow, How many rooms do you have in there?"

"I just love what you have done with this house."

Bill, with puffed up chest, winks and smiles wide as he accepts the compliments of his now beloved "Old Blue," as he affectionately calls her.

I smile and wink up at God.

By wisdom a house is built and through understanding it is established.

Through knowledge it's rooms are filled with rare and beautiful treasures.

Proverbs 24:3-4

Now it was really happening; we were really on our way. Yes, we ended up purchasing a big blue house that we had admired by the beach without much thought but rather on a wing and a prayer. We were off to that small town very far away. Bill and Jack led the two-car caravan. Hadley and I, with the dog, trailed behind in the rain. Cars were packed, doors locked—good-bye city life. I never looked back for fear of turning into a pillar of salt.

Thinking back, while travelling toward our new frontier, I realized that the big city was just a different way of life. The city life has been referred to something similar to that of being on a treadmill or living in a rat race. It just has an incredible pace, and you find yourself living it accordingly. You must keep up or be run over. It is also common knowledge that city people tend to have no manners or are a bit rude. It is not a matter of being vindictive or cruel. It is just extra hard to be nice when everyone is moving so fast around you. But those of us who are from the city know that it isn't that we have no manners and such. We just have a different mindset and different virtues. Our pure arrogance and snobbery help to make us the charming sophisticates that we are. Yet somehow, I knew that this way of life was getting in the way and hindering me from helping Hadley.

Yes, the rules are quite different in the city. Take a simple, normal task like driving an automobile for example. In the big city, everyone knows that the rule is eat or be eaten—every man for himself. Anytime you head out behind that wheel, you know that it will be a challenge. You say to yourself, may the best man win. The number one rule is to never make eye contact—especially if you are the least bit sensitive. You just never know what offensive sign language you might encounter.

Equally important is the rule that one does not slow down or stop for yellow lights. Everyone knows that this is your second chance to make it through the intersection. You just treat it as though the yellow light is green. Now if you forget that rule, no need to worry. There will most likely be two or three knowledgeable drivers behind you, type-A personalities, to promptly beep you through. They will beep repeatedly, loudly, and obnoxiously to remind you so that you will remember the rule, and you will not make that mistake again. While driving in the city, you will play by the rules.

Quite the contrary in a small town...

I loved our new small town, but, as I said earlier, it took about a year to shake off the rules of living in the city. It was quaint, clean, and quiet. The downtown was easy enough to maneuver. I found that I could get to several establishments all within minutes of each other. At times I wondered if a bomb had gone off and annihilated half of the population.

There were hardly any cars on the road, especially during what should have been rush hour. I no longer had to give myself forty-five minutes to travel a quarter mile to get a half-gallon of milk. Three months now, settling in, I could feel the outer layer was finally coming off, or so I thought. Proud of myself, venturing out daily to familiarize myself with my new surroundings, was when it happened.

I happened to be stopped at a red light on the main street in the center of town. I was engrossed in the southern hullabaloo coming from the one and only station that would tune in on my car radio. I noticed that the light had changed to green, but I just sat there. Another half a second and still no movement; I just sat there. I could feel myself slipping back to the old me as I thought, *Has the earth stopped rotating? Why were we not moving?*

My foot was pulsating off of the break. It was impatiently waiting to make its move. It was ready to put the pedal to the metal. I took another look at the light. Yes, sure enough it was green and green means go. The car in front of me just sat there. I couldn't believe it. This kind of inconsiderate behavior just didn't happen where I came from.

I took a closer look only to find to my shock and dismay that the man in front of me was just sitting there, reading the paper. I exploded! The guy sat there reading a paper, oblivious to the fact that he was holding up traffic. I had contested that this was the most preposterous thing that could ever happen. Okay, for sure I was no longer in Kansas, much less the city where I had come from where civilized people existed.

What planet am I on? I thought.

I did the only thing I knew to do. I did the right thing. I promptly laid on the horn like there was no tomorrow.

I'll show him. After all, I am from a big city. Doesn't he know that I am important? I've got things to do and places to go. How dare he, a small-town man, of no importance, trump up my day and my precious time? I asked myself.

Then I caught a glimpse of my frenzied face in the rear view mirror.

Whoa, Nellie, I thought as I came back to my new small-town sensibilities. I had to remind myself where I was. *This kind of behavior doesn't belong here!* I chided. *What's my hurry anyway? Remember, we came here to slow down*, I scolded myself. *Still so close to the surface*, I thought to myself.

Gosh, I mused, *how could Hadley ever get well when I am so sick?*

Three weeks later I would get my answer, as I stood face-to-face with the man I had spitefully judged rude. Sunday morning the family and I were making our way through the parking lot of a local house of worship to attend services. I noticed one of the cars in the lot that looked hauntingly familiar. There it was right in front of me! How could I ever forget that car? It seemed to have sat in front of me that dreadful day for what seemed like an eternity! I knew every scratch, every inch of it. Oh no, not an encounter. That's not supposed to happen. This doesn't happen in the big city. Everyone knows that it is perfectly okay to take your frustrations out on anyone who happens to be in your way. Others may call it rude, but we know, being from the city, that it is just part of our everyday life. You just pound your fist with a darn straight kind of attitude. That's how we release our stress and everyone knows that. You can even make a mean face occasionally at someone because you know that you will never run into that person ever again. Not in a million years. Not in a million years, that is, if you continue to live in the big city.

That Sunday morning, the small town and its rules helped me to learn my first lesson in humility.

"Welcome," said the face of the rude man who had been reading the paper so comfortably in his car.

"You must be new around town," he said sincerely.

I gulped. How did he know? How could he tell? I felt my face grow hot and red. I was readying myself for a lecture or a scolding. Perhaps, even an extended offensive gesture; after all, I deserved it. Instead, much to my citified surprise, he gave me a friendly wink.

"Come on in, we're glad you're here," he said.

I breathed out a nervous breath and sheepishly walked in. That encounter is one I will never forget. Here I was ranting all of the time because of how others had treated Hadley so poorly. What about the treatment that I had dished out to this unsuspecting man? I was no better than all of the rest. The mercy and forgiveness bestowed upon me that morning was just the beginning of the kind of love and affection that would soon enrich not only my life but also Hadley's.

Because of this display of love and gentleness, she would gradually start to come back to us. I knew right at that moment that we had made the right choice to move here. I figured that if this town could tolerate me, and all of my issues, certainly they would embrace my Hadley. The actual move from one place to another in and of itself moved me in a valuable way. It was the beginning of the change and healing in all of us. While perusing my sweet town, I never beeped my horn again. We really believed that Hadley would be tolerated, nurtured, and accepted in this small town. We had no idea that we were in as much need as her.

The move became much more significant than a mere story about a traffic incident.

As time marched on in that small town, the people became more familiar with us and we with them. We began to trust one another. They began to accept us as we let down our walls. I reckon, even after twenty years, we will still be referred to as that nice new family that came here from that big city.

But we were finally settling in. One new ritual we found ourselves engaging in was the process of leaving the house a half hour early to shop but not because of the dreaded traffic. No, this was so we could socialize and make merry with anyone we would encounter in the grocery store. During any given shopping excursion, we would run into at least a half a dozen people that we knew. It was an amazing thing. This kind of thing was unheard of in the big city. People would just stop their shopping carts and simply chat and make pleasantries with one another.

What a great, built-in, peer-relationship program that would become for Hadley. She couldn't wait to go shopping because there was always someone their to banter with. And oh, how patient and sweet the people were to her. They never appeared to be too busy to stop and chat with Hadley. Shopping trips became social hours. On a rare occasion, if we didn't run into anyone, we found ourselves asking, "Hmm, I wonder where everyone is? There must be a school play tonight or maybe a basketball game." Oh how we loved our small town.

And not just the patrons but also, the employees were equally friendly. It was not uncommon to have such conversations as, "I read about your son making the honor roll," or "I sure love those daffodils you put in this year."

Gee, I thought, *all I was doing was buying a loaf of bread and a gallon of milk. People here sure seem to take an interest in you.*

This was kind of nice once you got used to it. People really cared about one another.

In a small town people are inherently connected. We are one. We are a family. Good or bad, we look out for each other. We keep each other in check. It took some time to get used to this surreal lifestyle. Do people really know more about us than we want them to? We shuddered. Maybe they know more about us than we do about ourselves. We laughed. But for the most part, we settled in and soaked it right up. Knowing that people cared about you was something that we needed a healthy dose of. What a place for Hadley.

Yes, Lord, your Word is true. You do work together the good for those of us who love you. You knew all along that we had to get to this place even if we came kicking and scratching. You were just waiting for us to obey. Obedience will lead to having your hand of favor upon us. Doors were beginning to open.

My life hangs in the balance, but I will not give up obedience to your laws.

Psalms 119:109

The Beach

Yes, the doors were beginning to open for us as we were acclimating to our new surroundings. I just wished that we could have closed them when the visitors came to town—I encountered the abominable sand monster or perhaps monster mom. I hadn't decided which.

With the United States sporting 95,000 miles of shoreline, it didn't seem to matter where we decided to play because we always managed to make a big splash. A steamy breeze stirred the curtains on the humid afternoon, serving up a blistering ninety-eight degrees. The kids were dripping with perspiration, looking up at me through pleading, soggy eyes. I decided to put away the rest of the chores for the day, and I announced, "We are going to the beach!"

One hour later, squeals of joy erupted from two sweet, lovable kids. We were finally free to carelessly romp the sandy corridor. What an amazing place we had moved to.

We now lived two blocks from the grandest stretch of beach in the state. The luscious air and sparkling waters cooled temperatures and raised attitudes in a hurry. Life on a beach—it just doesn't get any better than this. I began to relax and settle back in my sand chair and relish chapter three of *The Chronicles of Narnia*. The sun felt like it was baking my body to a golden brown while at the same time warming me on the inside and reaching down to the very depths of my soul. I couldn't remember when I had been so relaxed. For me there was nothing like the warmth of the sun to completely take me away temporarily from all of life's worries. If only that moment could have lasted forever.

"That is not yours!" rang the sound of an angry voice that I could not recognize.

It was the shrill of what appeared to be some sort of wild animal that had been illegally poached. *What could this intrusion to my peaceful solitude be?* I sighed. *Oh, Lord, where is Hadley? I must have taken a short leave of my senses.*

Who was I trying to kid? Did I forget for a moment with whom I had come to the beach with? Did I forget that I was not at home in the safe zone? How could I have taken my eyes off her for even a minute? My mind was frantic as I cried out for my Hadley.

I tossed my novel into the sand as I launched myself out of my chair. I expertly transformed my body and legs into what would be Olympic form. That's when I spotted her. Hadley had meandered off to a small group of little girls. Within seconds, I was in the middle of a scene and it was unbelievable. Another invisible hammer was taking a plunge at my already shattered heart! *Can't we just come to the beach like everyone else?* I cried. *Can't she just play with other kids like everybody else?*

Was I really witnessing this? I could not believe it. Right there, on the sugary sand, stood a grown woman towering over and screaming at my child. I stared in disbelief; though my feet felt like they were mounted in cement, my lungs and mouth were free and worked well.

"Hey!" I shouted. "What's going on here?"

Then I thought to myself, *Did Hadley hurt someone? Did she break something? Did she eat someone's snack?*

The beastly animal turned its fixed, glazed eyes from Hadley to me. Hadley dropped the toy she held on to upon the sand.

"How dare your child just take my child's toys? She didn't even ask us!"

So this is what this is all about? I cried with relief, grateful that it wasn't something worse. I uttered a nervous laugh. And still trying to understand the obvious overreaction of the woman, I looked frantically from her to Hadley. Trying to quickly assess the situation. I assumed that Hadley, not knowing how to ask, simply helped herself.

"Mom," cried the other little girl, "it's okay. We don't mind if she plays with us."

After several pleas from the obviously embarrassed little girl, she gave up trying to sway her mom as if this were another defeated battle. Still standing there on the sand, confused as to whom to address first, in what seemed like hours of suspended time, an angel out of nowhere appeared to my much-needed rescue. My helpless, four-and-a-half- year-old child just stood defenseless right there, at the beach, oblivious to a not-so-tolerant world. She had no idea what all the commotion was about. I took Hadley by the hand and started walking away.

The angel woman called to me and, with a gentle sincerity, said, "Ma'am, I saw the whole thing."

This person out of nowhere, this angel, began to explain to me what she had witnessed from a few beach chairs away. Apparently, Hadley had been watching two little girls frolicking and playing with blow-up alligators and other assorted water toys. This angel went on to summarize that since Hadley hadn't been invited to join in and the temptation being too great of wanting so much to play, she decided to take matters into her own hands. So in Hadley fashion, not understanding the rules, not being able to speak or negotiate the appropriateness of asking first, she dove right in.

I concurred with her assumption and explained that in Hadley's world it is perfectly normal to plunge right in and join the fun whether invited or not. For her it is a "what's yours is mine" kind of attitude. Boundaries have no limits. I explained that this was one of the toughest lessons we were trying to teach to our autistic child. Hadley had a real problem with asking first, before just taking what did not belong to her. The angel went on to say that the other two little girls didn't seem to mind the intrusion. Little kids just seem to have more tolerance for differences.

The angel woman reported that the monster mom

seemed completely out of line in overreacting the way that she did. Seeing the whole thing, knowing that I was engrossed in my book, the stranger wanted to make sure that I knew what had taken place and was willing to help defend me and my child in any way if necessary.

I thanked her, smiled with gratitude, and assured her that I would be okay. By now I was quite rehearsed in making my apologies for greater atrocities wherever they occurred, be it the beach, the grocery store, the school, the world. The angel mom nodded her head in an understanding way.

As for the monster, this mom didn't hold the same beliefs as the angel mom or even her own daughter. She didn't seem to understand the value of sharing or even being kind. I supposed that it was because Hadley was different. She looked normal but something was not quite right. She made grunting sounds instead of talking. She flapped her arms like a bird and occasionally walked on her toes. Obviously such barbaric etiquette would condone any mom to ward off, keep away, from her very normal, very fortunate, undamaged child. The angel mom gave me a confident look as she left. She shot a "shame on you" look over to the *momster* to imply that the child just wanted to play. Her look implied, "How could you be so cruel to this curious, somewhat different, but friendly, child?"

I turned from this unfortunate day on the beach with a sobbing child in tow and gathered up our stuff. It was heartbreaking because Hadley just couldn't understand what all the commotion was all about. She had come to the beach full of want and anticipation to play like any other child. Why did there always seem to be so much stress, anxiety, and drama everywhere we went? While picking up the last of our towels, the monster mom launched her final missile. I actually felt bad for her as she stood there because it was as if she wanted to say something but just didn't know what. Possibly she was feeling some remorse. Maybe she had just had a bad day. Maybe she had an experience with someone stealing her child's stuff. *I need to let her off the hook*, I thought. But I was doubtful as I heard her jeer sarcastically, "What's her problem anyway?"

"She's autistic," I replied with a lump in my heart and throat the size of a boulder. Then I turned toward her and fired back with every ounce of courage I could muster. "Her problem is autism," I repeated. "What's yours?"

Of course, all the way home, I blamed myself because I should not have taken my eyes off Hadley for even a minute. I knew better. It is so hard to be a parent of an autistic child because you are constantly torn between guiding their every move and letting them try things on their own. It never seemed to fail that whenever I got too comfortable and didn't pay full attention, something would get out of hand.

Remember, these were the early days of our plight. Hadley was not being properly treated and I was depressed. We were very new to our community and did not know many people. Years later we would discover the spot on the beach where the locals hung out. It was there that we could safely play because people knew us and were tolerant. But until that time, we were right there in the mix with other visitors on the beach who just didn't know or understand us. Hadley's conduct was still viewed as unpredictable, as we were not yet administering supplements or gluten-free foods. Her bizarre habits were manifested by what was going on for her physically. My demeanor as well was unpredictable. I shouldn't have let my guard down for a minute. Oh, how I could have easily engaged Hadley in play and gently involved the other little girls. I could have explained that Hadley had special needs but likes to play just the same as them. Why, always, in hindsight do we see our mistakes? I was still somewhat in denial of Hadley's autism and not doing a very good job of letting go of my own anger.

All the way home we were both sobbing as I assured Hadley that we would go to the beach tomorrow and have a much better day. *Could she possibly understand any of this?* I wondered. Her large, brown, despondent eyes indicated that she understood and that crushed my soul. *Lord, please*, I prayed, *give me discernment, knowing how and when to pick my battles. When will I ever learn? Help me to keep my mouth shut and to try to do the right thing no matter what. Please help me to focus on Hadley's needs right now. Give me the strength to put aside mine.*

In all fairness to the visitors who came, the beach was really a great place, and a great time had by all. This was just one isolated, unfortunate encounter during what I refer to as the dismal years. Though it was unbearable at the time, I have completely forgiven the woman in my heart. I honestly don't know for sure if I would have been any different if the tables had been turned. My acceptance to tolerance has been so stretched since I have been living with someone who requires so much grace. That goes for me as well as Hadley.

Now then, back to the beach. I, being originally from the big city, enjoy meeting new and interesting people, and many we did meet right there on that glorious beach. Many were very inclusive with their activities and allowed Hadley to join in the fun. Others remarked at how well we seemed to manage her considering the disabilities.

"What a nice job you are doing with your daughter," they would remark after Hadley would promptly mutter a thank you for something that was offered to her.

There was even one time when we were casually building our sand castle and found ourselves in quite a predicament. Hadley and I were putting the finishing touches on our splendid castle when suddenly it occurred to me to check on Jack. I looked up and spotted him swimming out just a little bit too far. He was having fun but getting just a little too close to in over his head.

"Stay right here, Hadley," I instructed. I sprang to my feet and headed toward the water's edge. As I waded in ankle deep, I yelled for Jack to come back in. "This way, Jack, you are out too far."

At the same time, I darted my eyes back twenty feet to where I had left Hadley and the sand castle. The castle was standing tall but Hadley was gone. *Oh Lord*, I cried, as I scanned the sunbathers. I finally spotted her bright, pink swimsuit and golden pigtails running toward the snack shack, which happened to be a hundred yards away.

"Hadley!" I yelled at the top of my lungs from the water's edge.

"Where on earth has she decided to go?" I shrieked.

She was headed right for the snack shack where there were hundreds of people. Any other child might be fine, but this was Hadley. I was sure to lose sight of her from where I stood. Could she be trusted to be safe? Would she go away with a stranger if asked? I turned a panicked look back to my son who was frolicking neck deep.

"Jack, come back in, you are out too far! Oh, Lord," I cried. My son, my daughter, whom do I go after? Talk about "Sophie's choice." Whom do I save? I cried aloud.

There I was on the cold water's edge, literally arms stretched out as far as the east is from the west, trying to grasp my kids who were both equally in danger and fifty yards apart! That's when the lady on the beach came running over to my rescue.

"Ma'am, I have four kids of my own, and I can see the dilemma that you are in. Go get your son and I will retrieve your little girl."

No argument there. I dashed farther into the cold water. I waded out far enough to call out to Jack so he could hear me. Minutes later, we approached the sandcastle, dripping wet. We saw Hadley skipping happily hand-in-hand with the rescue lady back toward us. The Lord sure does know all about the extra help that I need with my special child, and he delivers!

In my distress I prayed to the Lord, and the Lord answered me and set me free.

Psalms 118:5

Sideliners

One really neat benefit of living so close to the beach is that you get to walk to it. You don't have to drive to it. You don't have to put up with whining kids as you circle the beach parking lot three or four times in an overheated van in hopes of finding a place to park. You don't have to try to squeeze into overcrowded sardine like spots provided risking dings and car jams.

People who don't live close to the beach are forced to drive to it in order to get to enjoy it. People who live far away from the beach have to work real hard all year long in order to spend one precious week here, two if they're lucky. They come to enjoy the splendor of one of God's most treasured gifts to mankind, and that is the beach.

The warmth of the sun, the sugary sand, and the inviting, frothy waves lure people back year after year. Long-standing friendships have been established over the years at the beach. The same old faces return year after year to survey the anticipated, breathtaking sunsets. Many a romance has been ignited at the beach. The actual beach itself becomes a luxurious, tropical habitat. Each year people who live far from the beach come to their familiar spots to relax, restore, and mend their souls. I've come to notice that these spots even have ownership by those who come.

"Mom, where should we throw the blankets?" said the young tourist.

"Over there, honey, you know, our usual spot," declares the visiting mom.

Now that we live close to the beach, we have observed that it is occupied by all kinds of different people. There are those who annoy us by spewing unwanted vulgar language. They quench their thirst with way too much alcohol and at the same time carelessly litter and trash the beach.

There are the families with small children who come sporting picnic baskets, buckets of sunscreen lotion, and assorted beach toys. They tend to migrate toward other families with small children to insure safe, fun, social, interactive playtime with other kids.

Then there are the teenagers. They usually try to find a somewhat secluded, out-of-the-way spot to blast their tunes, toss their Frisbees, and allow their hormones to wildly flap in the wind.

The older generation prefers the shadier spots of the beach under the trees found closer to the parking lot, as opposed to the water's edge. They tend to bring high-back lawn chairs (never a low-to-the-ground sand chair) and multicolored umbrellas. Not to mention that it is obviously the closest spot to the bathhouse.

Nevertheless, I've noticed that each group has their own spot conducive to their wants, needs, and desires.

We locals, those of us who live close to the beach, have our own territory. It is strategically nestled up against the dune and just far enough away from the visitors. We all know one another. It flows. It is safe. The kids are allowed to play with one another even if they are somewhat different. Since everyone knows each other, differences are tolerated.

As I stated at the beginning of the story, we live here so we walk to the beach. Walking to and from the beach is a daily ritual during the summer as we live two short blocks away from it. Later I will tell of an unusual walk home from the beach. Since we here we have beach paraphernalia down to a science. We have everything from goggles and flippers to rafts and inner tubes. Toys and towels are packed, stowed neatly in a tote bag, and ready to go. In one fell swoop, we can gather up the kids and the essentials and be on our way to the beach in a moments notice. We have everything that we need to last the entire day for frolicking in the sun.

A good part of our day is spent at the beach during our summers, so much so that we often refer to it as our recreation room. We can frequent the beach as much as our hearts' desire and do so simply because we can. Elvis and Gidget have nothing on us. And yet at the end of the day, it is the hardest thing in the world to get those kids to leave the beach. As if they thought somehow that they might not get another chance to return. As the day comes to an end, much to the kids' dismay, with the sun beginning to drop and the sunburns sizzling, the day must end and it is time to go home.

It was now time to leave our safe haven, our safe spot on the beach, and begin our walk home. By now the entire beach was packed with people who did not live close to the beach. These people did not know us. They especially didn't know my special child. We now entered what I call the battle zone as we wound our way through crowded sidewalks with special child in tow. As we meandered through unknown territory, I could almost feel our safe, protective shield melting away. *There is bound to be trouble*, I said to myself, dreading the walk home.

The abnormal conduct of an autistic girl, tolerated and accepted by local people who know us, may not be acceptable to the visitors. I can't help but describe them as anything other than the enemy. In enemy territory the definitions for characterizing people can vary. What was once considered a very special child is now proclaimed as an unruly, spoiled brat. Since this very special child happens to look absolutely normal, the expectation for her behaving accordingly is assumed. So when the enemy witnesses this normal-looking child unleashing bizarre, unpredictable, random behavior, it is no wonder they hold unfair opinions. Opinions are often made by observations. There was one less opinion formed that hilarious day as no observation was made.

On that hot summer day while walking home from the beach in enemy territory, an unnoticed event occurred. My special child and I were trudging along through the crowded streets. We had only a few more unsafe, unfamiliar spots to pass through. We were almost there. We were going to make it. Then it happened, a temptation too great to pass up.

An opportunity waiting to unfold was upon us. My children and I were squeezing our way through the crowded sidewalk along the beach. Jack and his friends were just ahead of us carrying the towels and sand buckets while Hadley followed behind wearing the blow up inner tubes. There in front of us, directly in our path, was a typical crowd of visitors deep in vacation fracas mode. One of the unsuspecting visitors, the one with the itsy-bitsy polka-dotted bikini was so engrossed in her conversation that she didn't have awareness of her far-outstretched arm extended into a hungry pedestrian's path. That tanned, outstretched arm was holding a chocolate-frosted, dripping-ever-so-slowly, ice cream confection. It seemed to be just begging to be licked.

That was exactly what this special child assumed as she skipped along, trying to keep up the pace, donned in her large, yellow daffodil, water blow up on her head. The boys had stepped down off of the curb and went around the crowd, but not Hadley. To Hadley it couldn't have been more perfect. Instead of having the ability to make the appropriate response, such as, "Please excuse me," she thought, "An ice cream cone in my direct path, at mouth's level."

How lucky for me, her devious grin implied. *It's only normal to help yourself and have a bite*, she thought with surety. *"No one would mind"*—I could almost hear her saying this, as though I could read her thoughts. Then, without missing a beat and keeping the pace, donning that ridiculous costume, complete with giant daisy-shape inner tube encircling her tiny body, Hadley turned her head slightly to the left and took her bite.

She continued walking right in step while enjoying her treat. It couldn't have been staged better—what precision, what choreography! No one saw a thing except her distraught mother who was sweating profusely behind her and sucking in her teeth. Now with this type of special child you really have to pick and choose your apologies and your battles. I glanced down at Hadley and noticed the absolute, innocent bliss and satiated pleasure on her face and said, "*Not today.*"

Whew, I breathed and hurriedly redirected my cherub away from the ambushed cone and continued at a frenzied pace.

To my surprise, nobody shouted after us. There was no one demanding that we purchase another cone. No one even appeared to notice a thing. I continued to walk from the beach with my human daisy and wondered about the person who did not live close to the beach. What would she think when she finally stopped conversing and turned her attention back to lick her cone and discover that half of it was missing? I'll never know.

That human flower and I continued walking on home into the sunset. I thanked God for another day in paradise and thought, there really are a few advantages to being *special* and living so close to the beach.

The land you have given me is a pleasant land. What a wonderful inheritance.

Psalms 16:6

Holidays

Christmas

There is no place like home for the holidays…

This was the Christmas before we moved to that big old blue house that I begged Bill to buy for me. We hadn't planned on moving into that house until later in the spring. It not only had junk left behind from the previous owners but it was quite dilapidated and in need of much repair. We figured that we would work on it slowly over the spring and make our permanent move by the end of May. However, life in general was going from bad to worse back home in our big city and we wanted to get out of Dodge. So we packed up the kids and the dog and headed north for a Christmas getaway.

Our soon to be a new home was only two short blocks

from the opulent beach. We had only hung out in this small town inclusive of its majestic seashore during the summer months so we had no idea of what to expect in December. We were amazed to find how a warm, sunny seaside coastal town could be instantly transformed from a tropical playground into a dreamy wintry wonderland overnight through the changes of the season.

As we continued north the temperature steadily dropped but that massive ocean like body of water appeared to lend a snug, cozy white, warm blanket of insulation enveloping this small town. A deep sub zero temperature, sixty-mile per hour winds and a mere four feet of freshly fallen snow greeted us that winter. That is what our family faced as we pulled off of the highway and on to our exit that first uncharted Christmas.

"Wow," Jack said, as we slowly navigated the up north snow pack streets.

"Is this the same place that we visit in the summer? Cuz it sure looks like the North Pole to me."

When we finally reach our neighborhood and tried to pull into the driveway we were faced with a three foot white giant wall of snow.

Hadley and I waited patiently in the car for about a half an hour while Bill, in snow up to his thighs and Jack up to his neck, shoveled out a spot so we could pull into the drive. The boys, thoroughly exhausted, finally finished moving the snow and tossed their shovels into the huge, white mountain that they had created.

"That's good buddy boy," Dad said as he rubbed his aching back. Lets' get the car into the drive and the girls out of the car and have some fun."

It had been a four-hour drive and this would be a great way to stretch our tired, sore muscles.

What merriment we enjoyed while playing in the fluffy mile-high banks of snow that night. "I guess kids will be kids no matter what," I said to myself.

Because of her autism I was a bit uncertain as to how Hadley would respond to the cold marshmallow playground we found ourselves in. Much to my surprise, she shot out of the car faster than lightning and threw herself into the white bank in pure delight and wonderment. No tactile issues here from my autistic child, I thought.

"Yeah', one small step for mankind, or was it autistic-kind," I joked aloud referring to Hadley.

"We must be at the North Pole," Jack said again as he gazed up to the sky with his head stretched far back as it could without it falling off of his neck.

"Cuz I can almost reach up and grab those bright shiny stars." He continued.

I couldn't agree more, I thought as I glanced up at the crystal clear galaxy brilliantly twinkling and dancing above our heads on the very dark, rich black canvas.

> When I look up at the sky and see the works of your fingers,
> The moon and the stars that you set in place
> What are mere mortals that you should think about us?
>
> *Psalms 8:3*

"We certainly are not in Kansas anymore, much less the big city we came from," I teased. "I've never witnessed the sky so clear."

When I glanced back down from gazing at the stars I saw Hadley's serene face gazing up at the constellations or maybe heaven itself as her tiny body lay there in the snow. She was flexing her little self into a snow angel, seemingly normal and without a care in the world. She evidently expressed no vexation to the cold wet snow.

Although she had no speech at the time her eyes appeared to be communicating with a heavenly being.

What a sight on that eve of Christmas Eve. It was a moment of unexpected normal—no meltdowns, no screaming and crying for no apparent reason. It was just a little girl, rolling, playing and eating snow right along with her big brother. To this day I consider that moment a Christmas gift from God, nothing short of a Christmas miracle.

Dear God, I thought, *could my baby really be an angle wrapped up in human clothing?* I silently pondered that thought in my heart as I breathed into the frigid night air.

"Better come on into the house now," Bill called from the back door, the sound of his voice transporting me from cloud nine back to the planet.

"But you might want to leave your coats on," he continued. "I've been tinkering with the heater in the basement—it was making some weird noises. It doesn't appear to be giving out much heat either. It might be a long cold night!"

And that was just how it happened that first eve of Christmas Eve. The four of us plus the dog ended up hunkered down for a long winters nap in our soon to be new home.

It turned out that our bedroom was the warmest room in that big old barn. It was a master suite that fortunately was complete with a king-size bed. It offered plenty of room for all us as we nestled together as one that chilly night.

As Bill had predicted there would be very little heat from the antique furnace and it was definitely on the fritz. I instructed Bill that a modern unit would replace it, of the 21st century vintage to be sure, after the first of the year.

But eventually, our hearts and souls began to thaw the next day as we bravely explored our new frontier. We tried our best to transform that cold, enormous, empty, wanting so much to be loved, facade of a home into a cozy, warm safe sanctuary.

Though she was being a real good sport, Hadley's routine had been completely disrupted by this spontaneous get-a- way. We needed to create a structure. Hadley depends on structure for survival like most of us depend on air in order to breathe.

We were still reeling from the diagnosis of autism given to Hadley as well as the question of how do we fit into a world that doesn't seem to have a place for us?

I guess you could say that we just ran away from our troubles that Christmas, at least temporarily, for a few restful weeks.

We had decided to run for the hills. We grabbed our Christmas cards, our boxes and packages along with our tattered cartons of bulbs, ribbons, holly, and mistletoe and headed up north.

The Christmas season taxes the sanest of folks, but multiply that by ten if you are living with autism. Normal routines are abruptly changed; Dailey structured events completely spoiled, unanticipated people and family members resembling polite strangers visiting with out warning, Then there are the events; sitting for long periods of time at concerts, pageants and various other holiday performances. Not to mention the market place: the loud holiday music blasting throughout normally quiet shops, festive bright lights blinking off and on, jam-packed malls and sidewalks; all granted, most of us normal folks love it—a complete nightmare for the autistic child.

For the next few days we tacked up wreaths, holly and strung up multi-colored lights. We taped our Christmas cards to the spacious vestibule in the parlor. There is no place like home for the holidays, even if it was our makeshift "home away from home."

Life would definitely be slower here and the best part being we would be undisclosed.

We had no history, yet, only a past, and it was temporarily behind us at least for the next couple of weeks.

Those two weeks were nothing short of living within a Tomas Kincaid calendar. Our Victorian house was not only two blocks from the beach but it was also walking distance to the main street of our picturesque little town.

The next morning we decided to walk into town and

have a bite to eat. We passed other Victorian style homes on our way. These magnificent homes were embellished with freshly fallen powdery snow. Yards were landscaped with tall evergreen trees drooping with heavy snow laden branches adorning crimson holly.

The downtown consisted of about six blocks east and west intersecting with a crossroad that extended four miles moving north and south. Radiant lights beamed from the frosted festive quaint gift shops windows.

Continuing towards main street, we passed a small city park, along with a Dairy Bar and Grill that appeared to have been there for decades. At the center of town stood proudly a stately three-story clock. To the east was an age-old scarlet red limestone Court House. Dignified, ornamented lampposts marked off each and every block along the main street.

Our undisclosed quirky outrage moved along the quiet streets of town like concealed tourist out of season. Jack and Bill were running and sliding down the slick streets in their tennis shoes. If our dubious daughter didn't give us away proving us to be abnormal folks, then certainly the boys would donning their out-of season clothing.

We were in the land of the Tundra people, nothing like blowing our cover the first day.

I thought that I had noticed a shoe store up the street. We would definitely be stopping in there after lunch to be properly out-fitted for Northern style-boots, and other up-north attire.

Allured by the festive windows the boys were pointing and commenting on all the wares that they were exposed to.

"How about the 'Rome Total War' this year Jackie boy," Bill asked. "It is a new computer game. I hear it is lots of fun, plus it teaches you about history," Bill explained.

"That sounds great Dad, though I sure wish we could find something this year that would include Hadley," Jack added thoughtfully.

Hadley was doing exceptionally well trying to keep her clumsy gait while navigating the icy streets. She would point at toys and make small attempts at words to express her excitement, as if imitating her brother, seemingly wanting so much to communicate with us.

"What is she trying to say?" I desperately asked to no one in particular. "She wants to tell me so bad what it is that she wants, but I can't understand her," I mourned.

I caught a glance of my despondent face in the reflection of the happy Christmas window as the skater figurines completed their figure eights.

"Mary, this looks like a cozy place for breakfast," Bill yelled out to me from the diner he and Jack were standing in front of.

Yes, I nodded in agreement as I filed my emptiness into the recesses of my broken heart and headed towards my family.

We finished our breakfast at the diner that prided it self in baking homemade bread and serving up lumberjack portions of eggs, hash brown and bacon.

"Well that sure hit the spot; and it sure beats the heck out of tofu and yogurt for a change," Bill demonstrated as he rubbed his hand over his stuffed belly.

After breakfast our next stop, meandering through the

town, we approached the enormous early 1900'S Style clock fixed in the town center. Low and behold, we stumbled upon good ole St. Nick himself. There he was gaily sitting upon a large red velvet throne in the middle of an elf like village.

How perfectly festive, I thought. This town really goes all out on the gala decorations for the holidays. Here is my chance to capture a holiday Kodak moment, I rejoiced.

But remembering the horrors of the past, *Would Hadley cooperate?* I worried.

Heck, for all I know Jack will be the one to have a meltdown this time since he flat-out told me last year that there would be no more pictures of him and the jolly arctic man.

Much to Jack's dismay, including a lot of tugging and warring, and a surprisingly, curiously cooperative Hadley, I got my picture of the two kiddo's up on Santa's lap.

Snap. Snap.

Wow, she is still sitting up there on Santa's lap, I marveled as I shot my camera. Last year she would have nothing to do with this charade.

But when that jolly old man looked tenderly into Hadley's eyes and asked her what she would like Santa to bring her for Christmas she just sat there mute.

"Oh dear," I guess I was fooling my self into thinking that things would be different, that maybe things would be normal this time.

How to explain to this jolly man? I sighed to myself. And then I began my nervous dance of fretting, gesturing, and finally yelling out suggestions that any normal little girl of her age might ask.

Say something, Hadley, anything, I silently pleaded to myself.

Silence.

"She would like to have the Thomas the Tank Engine," I offered timidly.

"She would like a doll that eats and wets her diaper," I continued a bit louder and with surety.

"She would like a Lamb Chop doll!" I shouted out in exasperation.

Silence.

I was still too embarrassed to tell family, friends, strangers, much less a Santa, that this beautiful little girl was not normal. I couldn't bring myself to say the word... *AUTISM*. I couldn't bring myself to admit to him that my precious baby sitting on his lap was autistic so she couldn't tell him what it is that she wants for Christmas, or for any other time for that matter!

The Santa man scratched his head and glanced at me sideways, obviously reacting to *my* over reacting.

"She is just a bit shy," I offered as my best excuse.

The Santa man seemed to sense my anguish that my foreboding behavior conveyed. He gave me a reassuring glance as if to say, "Don't worry Mom, this happens all of the time. Take it easy."

Then the patient man asked gingerly once again.

"It's ok little girl, don't be shy. Now tell Santa what you would like to have for Christmas."

Silence.

Hadley willingly sat there mute.

She sat there contented and at ease while staring into his eyes. She didn't appear to be afraid but instead sort of mesmerized with his brightly red colored suit, rosy cheeks and extremely long, fluffy white beard. So much for the theory declaring that autistic kids do not make eye contact. She was doing intense battle on a stare down of who would blink first that I've ever witnessed.

Then she began softly patting his rosy cheeks with her tiny hand. She glanced at me with one of her infamous impish grins and then glanced back again at Santa.

"No, don't do it Hadley," I shrieked. "Please just tell the nice man what you want. PLEAASEE…"

Ignoring me she reached up and pulled Santa's furry white beard right off of his face, as if to see for her self if it was real. Was it just plain old curiosity or was it her inability to resist temptation of the immensely white fluffy visual that possessed her to reach up and have a feel, a touch? God only knows!

I hastily pulled Hadley off of the lap of the perplexed Santa while he hurriedly rearranged his obvious costume and his revealed identity.

To my amazement he began chuckling. He was actually chuckling aloud

He gave my Hadley a pass! That had been unheard of so far in her very young life.

"Ha…ha…ha," snickered the jolly old man.

"Kid you just made my day."

"Ha…ha…ha…" he continued laughing.

I began searching and darting my eyes all around in hopes that there were no other little kids to witness the girl of her age might ask.

Say something, Hadley, anything, I silently pleaded to myself.

Silence.

"She would like to have the Thomas the Tank Engine," I offered timidly.

"She would like a doll that eats and wets her diaper," I continued a bit louder and with surety.

"She would like a Lamb Chop doll!" I shouted out in exasperation.

Silence.

I was still too embarrassed to tell family, friends, strangers, much less a Santa, that this beautiful little girl was not normal. I couldn't bring myself to say the word… *AUTISM*. I couldn't bring myself to admit to him that my precious baby sitting on his lap was autistic so she couldn't tell him what it is that she wants for Christmas, or for any other time for that matter!

The Santa man scratched his head and glanced at me sideways, obviously reacting to *my* over reacting.

"She is just a bit shy," I offered as my best excuse.

The Santa man seemed to sense my anguish that my foreboding behavior conveyed. He gave me a reassuring glance as if to say, "Don't worry Mom, this happens all of the time. Take it easy."

Then the patient man asked gingerly once again.

"It's ok little girl, don't be shy. Now tell Santa what you would like to have for Christmas."

Silence.

Hadley willingly sat there mute.

She sat there contented and at ease while staring into his eyes. She didn't appear to be afraid but instead sort of mesmerized with his brightly red colored suit, rosy cheeks and extremely long, fluffy white beard. So much for the theory declaring that autistic kids do not make eye contact. She was doing intense battle on a stare down of who would blink first that I've ever witnessed.

Then she began softly patting his rosy cheeks with her tiny hand. She glanced at me with one of her infamous impish grins and then glanced back again at Santa.

"No, don't do it Hadley," I shrieked. "Please just tell the nice man what you want. PLEAASEE…"

Ignoring me she reached up and pulled Santa's furry white beard right off of his face, as if to see for her self if it was real. Was it just plain old curiosity or was it her inability to resist temptation of the immensely white fluffy visual that possessed her to reach up and have a feel, a touch? God only knows!

I hastily pulled Hadley off of the lap of the perplexed Santa while he hurriedly rearranged his obvious costume and his revealed identity.

To my amazement he began chuckling. He was actually chuckling aloud

He gave my Hadley a pass! That had been unheard of so far in her very young life.

"Ha…ha…ha," snickered the jolly old man.

"Kid you just made my day."

"Ha…ha…ha…" he continued laughing.

I began searching and darting my eyes all around in hopes that there were no other little kids to witness the revealing of the Santa impersonator.

"Oh the hearts that might have been broken or the shattered dreams of believers, all dashed in one fell swoop because we showed up," I bemoaned.

With lowered eyes I mumbled something about autism and carried Hadley rapidly down the street.

"That was awesome Hadley," Jack chortled.

"We don't do things like that Hadley," Bill scolded.

"Will it always be like this?" I lamented.

"I told you that we were too old to sit on Santa's lap," Jack laughed and hooted as we swiftly scurried down the street.

Later that afternoon the day was less eventful as we chose our Christmas tree out on an old farm.

We read the ad in the local paper about a tree farm telling how patrons could enjoy a hayride that would take you out on a tour of a variety of species of Christmas trees. The ad enticed that you could cut down your very own tree, enjoy refreshments, and even sing along to Christmas carols.

"Can we go, Mom? Can we?" Jack begged.

Yes, we were really going out to a farm to cut down our first Christmas tree. Even Hadley seemed to be excited as we tried to prepare her for the afternoon's event.

As promised in the ad we were given a hayride through the woods that were permeating the most intoxicating smell of pine. We sat mesmerized on the top of haystacks piled up on the rickety wagon. The massive farm offered magnificent rows of Douglas Firs, Blue Spruce, Frasiers, and Balsams. These trees stood at attention as if to be boasting their obedient stature. We were driven and pulled by four beautiful brown draft horses with thick, long dark manes.

With so many grand trees it would be difficult to decide.

After a half an hour and what seemed equivalent to that of World War II, Bill finally got his way. We ended up with that one hundred pound mammoth tree of his choice.

The experienced farmer gave a sigh as he hoisted that massive tree, helping Bill attach it to the roof of our car. The kids and I enjoyed hot cocoa, brightly iced sugar cookies, and listened to classic Christmas carols in the heated barn.

Getting the tree home was one problem. Standing it up in the parlor was another. The tree fell over and on to the floor three times before Bill decided to tie it up to the wall.

"What is it about things falling over and smashing to the ground that make Hadley laugh and laugh?" I wondered aloud.

Jack guessed that it was likened to that of a cartoon for her. "Everything bounces back in her world, Mom," he explained.

"Maybe," I sobbed, as I swept the shards of the last of my antique glass bulbs that had been smashed to smithereens from the tree crashing to the hard wood floors for the third time. Hadley continued to laugh and laugh.

Not bad for our first day in our soon to be new hometown. So far so good.

Exploring the small town prospects, check.

Breakfast and visit with Santa, check.

Christmas tree selected and dressed, check.

Only thing left to do was find a church to celebrate the reason for the season.

Silent night, Holy night
All is calm, All is bright...

We huddled together tightly in a pew near the back of the very small church that had been recommended to us.

The friendly man from the local shoe store had invited us to worship at his church for the Christmas Eve service. He had befriended us in a nice conversation while fitting the boys with boots and gear earlier that morning.

So much for being anonymous, we couldn't have picked a smaller congregation to celebrate the birth of our Savior. The church we attended back home had three or four thousand folks per service. Nothing like sticking out like sore thumbs, but at least we had the right boots this time.

Heavenly host sing, Hallelujah...

We sang out with heavy hearts and our heads held high along with that sweet little church that warmly welcomed us that night. Mr. Snyder acknowledged us with a gentle nod as he noticed that we had taken him up on his invitation.

Other kind men and women began to nod our way as well making us feel at ease and accepted. As if to imply, you must be new around these parts but we are glad that you are here. Bill was eventually able to loosen his monkey grip on Hadley, as she seemed to be miraculously calm and content.

All is calm, All is bright

Sleep in heavenly peace.

Oh how we had longed for a night of Heavenly peace.

And peace God sure did provide many a Christmas Eve to come as we settled into our new small town community living with autism. That glorious season seemed to come around faster and faster each year. Christmas became more and more significant to Hadley each year as she healed and came out of her autistic fog.

As she healed and continued evolving as a unique little person she even began to participate in Christmas activities. When Hadley was nine, she participated in all of the church and school plays. One of my favorite memories from Christmas' past was the year that Hadley landed an angel role in the church Christmas pageant.

"Next year I'm giving her a much bigger role," informed Mrs. McCrath. "Why she not only knows her own lines, but she can recite everyone else's in all three acts. It's getting to where the kids look at her for their lines during rehearsal instead of me, she continued.

"What amazing recall and memory she has," the director boasted.

Oh, how Hadley has kept all of us young through the years while celebrating the ancient Holy day. I guess that I will go on decorating the house till I am eighty years old because of Hadley's love and rigid structure of annual events.

Because Hadley is extremely structured the process must start promptly on the first Saturday in December and not be removed until the very last minute of the last day of the month. Hadley is old enough to help with this ritual now and I am under her careful eagle eye so I dare not try to skimp on any details. Like the one year when I was so tired and thought I could get by with one less box of ornaments.

"Hey Mom, where are all the sheep and shepherds that are usually placed around the manger," Hadley expertly noticed being missing.

Rats, I thought in utter amazement, *now I have to go down and get that heavy box of miscellaneous stuff that I thought I could get away with her not knowing. Fat chance with that kid.*

"YOUR TURN!" I called out to Bill as I pointed back down the stairs.

I also had to stop the practice of wrapping the gifts early and placing them under the tree ahead of time. Hadley just couldn't resist the temptation of the dazzle and brightly colored packages with all of their allure.

"Surely these treasure are all for me," her impish grin would imply.

And the one true way to be sure of that would be to take matters into her own little autistic hands, and that is exactly what she proceeded to do.

Hadley would find a black permanent marker and expertly cross off the name of any package bearing any other name than her own and promptly write 'Hadley' on them.

"That takes care of that," she cried with elation.
"Mom!" Jack hollered, "she did it again!"

For unto us a child was born…
Isaiah 9:6

Easter

If our hands are to be the hands of God…

The Old Testament is filled with examples of how God works by using people to grant compassion or get a job done. God is so filled with compassion for us, that he reveals it either directly from himself or through the action of others. In the most unlikely situations, he shows up for people. For example, while on the great exodus from Egypt, the Israelites found themselves at the water's edge. Though they didn't always live a life pleasing to God, he took great compassion on them. It appeared that there was no way out for them and yet God made a way. He parted the sea for them.

There were so many times and situations with Hadley and dealing with her autism that I needed God to make a way for us to safely pass through. Three thousand years later, though God is not here physically with us, I think that he continues to show us compassion through the lives of others.

His hands are still being used today. There are people

out there who are willing vessels to be used by God, designed specifically to offer compassion to others. It is as if these people just seem to be instinctually equipped with radar for compassion. The unlovely, the repudiated, and various other misfits automatically come into view on their screens. These people simply adjust their antennas and tune you in. They just naturally know how to be kind. They know how to be kind to the abnormal types. For them it is inherent. These instinctively equipped types of people are more often than not kids, generally aged ten or less. Jacob was six years old and was incredibly equipped with compassion. He was about to be used by God, whether he knew it or not at the time, to show compassion to a less fortunate person. Hadley appeared on his screen, but we wouldn't find out about that until later.

We had made it through our first warm summer and held on tightly through the blustery winter. Hadley was five now and eight months into her kindergarten class. Though she still had no coherent speech, she was slowly making adjustments to her new environment. And now we were anticipating all the hope and new life that the spring has to deliver.

Hadley just loves the holidays and Easter was no exception. She loves reading stories about the Easter bunny, coloring eggs, and of course the thrill of the festive egg hunt. This was Easter weekend, and we had just read the glorious ad in the newspaper inviting the public to come to the Easter egg hunt scheduled for this Saturday morning.

Oh, how we wanted to participate!

What's the big deal? It's just a simple Easter egg hunt.

What could go wrong with a bunch of kids having fun? you might ask.

But nothing was ever that simple for us anymore. It wasn't a question about the event. It was more the alarming question of to go or *not* to go.

On that warm, spring, Saturday morning, we ventured out. Little kids and frenzied parents were gathering on the courthouse lawn in anticipation of the awaited Easter egg hunt. Kids were donning bunny ears and tails and carrying pastel bags. The excitement was infectious. Parents chatted with each other as children squealed and frolicked. Oh, how I wished that we had made some friends over the winter. I sighed. To have someone who understood us would really be helpful about now. The line was three people deep all the way around the roped-off grassy area. Children were impatiently tugging away from death grips of already exhausted parents.

"In just a few more minutes," the announcer shouted, "we will begin the hunt." I watched and took in all of the fever of the festive holiday mood. I couldn't help but think that something was just not right. I hadn't noticed this kind of scene since I was a child. The euphoric atmosphere was surreal, yet something was wrong with this picture.

Having come from a metropolitan suburb, the only thing I was anticipating was the rush of the police to cuff hands and haul away bodies. After all, you are talking about an Easter egg hunt on a courthouse lawn! That was unheard of where we had come from. Where was the separation of the church and the state? Where were all the protesters representing every other religious group not involving bunnies? Where were all the non-religious people? Where were all the angry chants and gestures? Maybe things were different here. Could it be possible? Where am I? This sort of thing would never have been permitted where I had come from.

Contemplating all the above questions off in a zone for what seemed like an eternity, I didn't hear the start of the bell—the ringing of the bell that gave the children the permission to finally tear free from their parent's clutches.

"Now for the great moment that we all have been waiting for," called the announcer.

I felt myself being pushed and shoved as the kids took off like rockets. Suddenly, I snapped out of my daydream. I suppose it could be possible that a small-town community could really have a religious holiday celebrated on the courthouse lawn. I assured myself that everything was going to be all right. We could just relax and have a good time and go home. That's when I realized that Hadley was gone.

Now unlike the other children and their parents' explicit squeals and delight of the unfolding events, my concealed anticipation was not the same. Mine was quite different. My anticipation involved squeals of delight but with much anxiety. Where was my baby? Was she safe? Was she still here? Then the voice piped in loud and clear. The voice that came in loud and clear in my head. The familiar voice that was audible every time that our family ventured out of the safety zone of our own home. Anytime that we wanted to participate with the others we heard the voice. The voice was demeaning and hurtful, *You are now entering enemy lines. Don't you realize that something always goes wrong when you show up?*

You could always count on it ringing loud and clear.

Abnormal entering normal territory. You do not belong here. Who do you think you are?

I dreaded the thought that normal people would soon discover that we were not normal. I dreaded the dire looks. They would see that we did not fit in. Some may even, accidently, be mean or cruel. I lowered my eyes as I scurried about frantically, searching for my baby.

Hadley had successfully wriggled free from my monkey grip. My eyes darted around the area faster than the speed of light. My heart pounded like restless native's drums beating wildly. I had lost sight of her. Where could she be? The horrors that raced through my mind seemed devastatingly endless. Would she know to stay within the grassy area of the hunt? Would some stranger carry her off ? I was overwhelmed with the usual sick combination of paranoia and the idea of imminent danger that most parents of special children often experience. The simplest thing as an Easter egg hunt could go very bad in the matter of seconds for us. But not this time, something very special took place that would allow Hadley to feel part of things for the first time ever.

A huge sigh of relief came from deep within me. I spotted that cherub of a child gleefully squealing with arms flapping wildly in the wind. At a glance one might think that was a child like any other. She looked normal by all definitions. But if one were to really watch intently for more than a few minutes, the truth would be found out. The toe walking, the unfixed gaze, and the fragmented speech were all sure indications of a not-so-normal child. That day, I didn't care. I refused to let it bother me today.

I watched her as proudly as any of the other parents watched their children. A few seconds of normal. I treasured the beautiful moment in my heart. *This is what it may have been like, if not for...not now.* The moment was hers. Hadley had them fooled. Peer imitation to the best of her ability, smiling from ear to ear, she raced and fought for her fair share of holiday sweets.

She trotted from one side of the grassy area to the other in search for those brightly colored eggs. But Hadley being who she was, limitations and all, was not so successful in her quest. Each time she bent down to collect her treasure, there seemed to be a much swifter child with much more coordination than herself. They would expertly swoop down, snatch up the candy, stow it in their boodle, and be on to the next.

Still Hadley persevered and kept up her brave front. She didn't seem to mind too much that the children swirling around her held bulging bags of chocolate delights and she had none. She was as happy as a clam.

But it was all I could do to not jump in and rescue her. Let her get some candy. I wanted to scream! I wanted to be her knight in shining armor and save the day. She was so helplessly elated. She seemed so helpless and yet so happy that my heart ached as I watched. I wanted so much to help her. What could I do? What would the other parents think? We had heard it many times before. Her appearance looks normal. I could hear them sneer. "Why is that mother out there picking up eggs for her child? What kind of crazy mom is she? This is supposed to be for the kids."

But didn't they realize that this was no ordinary kid? I sighed.

Just as my heart was being ripped to shreds with the conflict of emotions at hand, God sent Jacob into Hadley's path to make a way. His radar was on and antennas in tune. As he approached Hadley, I recognized him from her kindergarten class. He seemed to have been watching Hadley from afar. He seemed to be aware that she had an empty bag. He seemed to be so in tuned to her disposition for such a young human being that it still crumbles me to the core of my being today.

I will never forget those warm, dark eyes blazing onto my Hadley's face as he gently approached her. Willfully, he opened his bag, without being told to, and allowed her to have as much from it as she desired. He didn't mind that Hadley only grunted at attempts to speak. He didn't seem to mind that she took three little spins and twirls around him. He smiled at her and waited patiently for her to finish her happy dance.

"Hope you are having fun, Hadley," he said. "Happy Easter."

At his young tender age, he could see that there was someone less fortunate than himself. The candy didn't seem to matter so much anymore. He genuinely recognized and accepted her as one of his friends. Amidst all the exhilaration around him, he noticed the need of another. He took the time and had the compassion to part the sea for Hadley. He certainly seemed to be the hands of Christ. This equipped type, disguised as kindness and compassion and wrapped up in a six-year-old's body, came to Hadley's rescue that day.

What a glorious thing happened to us all on that Easter weekend. We had made it through an event with little to no major problems. In fact it was one of the first times we actually felt included. Jacob gave up something simple of himself for someone else. Jacob's small act of kindness took care of Hadley's needs.

Don't forget to be kind to strangers, for some who have done this have entertained angels without realizing it!

Hebrews 13:2

Mary Ann Payne, M. A.

Our Little Runaway

One of the biggest fears of any parent is the thought of losing their child. Children have an uncanny ability to go when the spirit moves them. The littlest distraction of focused attention can trigger the inquisitive mind in a snap, and they can be out of your clutch within the matter of seconds. One of the biggest problems regarding the difficulties in dealing with Hadley in the early years was that of her wandering off. Three times our fears were put through the test with the first two events occurring before we left the big city.

It was a warm spring morning. The sun was generously penetrating its warmth upon us, shinning through our casement family room windows. Oh, how nice it was to finally open up the, for much too long, tightly closed winterized shutters. The winter months seemed to last forever. I couldn't wait to open everything up to let in some fresh spring air in order to clear out the musty stale of winter. It was a typical Saturday morning for our little family. We had indulged ourselves by allowing an extra hour of sleep because we didn't have to race off to be anywhere. Still lounging in our pajamas, we slowly began to stir around the house, leisurely planning our day. The coffee pot brewed the French roasted beans. This filled my senses with an incredible, rich aroma that helped to remind me of how much I loved lazy Saturday mornings. Jack, five, and Hadley, three, had planted themselves in front of the television to watch *Thomas, the Tank Engine* as they ate their Cheerio's.

"Thomas, you are being rather cheeky." Jack laughed. He scolded the naughty engine that always seemed to be caught up in some kind of mischief during the one-hour episode. Hadley appeared to concur with his remark as she pointed and grunted in amused agreement. Setting my empty coffee mug into the sink, I called out to Bill who was kicked way back in his favorite chair reading the paper.

"Hey, darling, don't forget about that mid-morning social that the neighborhood association has scheduled for today. We promised that we would bring some Danish custard cream and fresh strawberries," I reminded.

"Hey, Bill, I feel so energized this morning," I continued. "Why don't we tackle that rug downstairs since it is so nice out today? Besides we still have plenty of time before we have to be at the social."

Bill had that hopeless look on his face that implied, "Oh drat, the dreaded honey-do list. There will be no winning this battle."

He tossed his newspaper aside and got down on the rug by the kids and began to wrestle with Jack.

"You'll never be able to pin me down, Gordon. Ha! Ha! Ha!" Jack laughed. "I am Thomas, a very useful engine," he said primly, using the names he had renamed himself and Daddy from his favorite television show.

Hadley flapped her arms mirthfully around them, watching all of the jovial play but seemingly not able to fully join in on the fun.

As we worked in the downstairs playroom, pushing the heavy carpet cleaner back and forth, the kids trundled down the steps several times to watch us. They pulled out toys from their trunk to transport back upstairs. Our house was fairly kid friendly with a large play area up as well as downstairs. It was not unusual that at any given time we might be on one level and they would be on another. It seemed to work well as we would check on them every twenty minutes or so. The kids could play for hours by entertaining themselves. It was always quiet though, as only one of them could speak at the time. Nonetheless, they would play side-by-side together in the same room.

A couple of hours later, back aching a bit and bearing a pretty good sweat, Bill suggested that we take a break.

"Let's go check on the kiddos and grab a cool glass of water," he said as he wiped his wet brow.

"This is as good as it's going to get," he proclaimed. We had been over the downstairs playroom carpet twice with the cleaner and even I thought it looked 100 percent better than when we had started.

"Hey, big boy," Bill said as he was at the sink, filling

two glasses with cold water. "Where's the Had?"

"I dunno," Jack said as he pulled his train around the track. *Toot, toot,* his train blew. "I thought she was downstairs with you guys."

"Okay, big guy, I'll go back down and get her. Mom said something about having a snack."

"Hadley, where are you, baby girl?" Bill called down to the playroom. He continued looking in the laundry room, the workout room, and the storage area.

"Hmmm, she is definitely not down here," he concluded.

"Come and have a snack, you two. Jack is patiently waiting at the table, and I have some sliced apples," I said.

Bill came back into the kitchen alone. "Where is Hadley?" I asked.

"I didn't see her downstairs, but I will go up and get her. She must be up in her room," he insisted.

A few minutes later, a panicked Bill came rushing into the kitchen alone again, saying that he had checked all of the rooms upstairs but Hadley was nowhere to be found. That horrible feeling of nausea crept over me and I felt my knees start to buckle.

"Okay, well, she has to be in here somewhere," I snapped. "Come on, Jack, let's check all of the rooms on this floor, and Bill, you go out and look around the yard."

After frantically searching for what seemed like hopeless, empty hours suspended in time, the three of us all met up again in the kitchen without Hadley.

"Good God," I cried. "This is just ridiculous. She was right here in this house with all of us. Where on earth could she be?"

I continued to search our forty-five-hundred-square-foot home. Bill and Jack decided it was time to investigate the neighborhood and check down at the potluck social.

"Hey, there you guys are! What took you so long to finally show up?" one of our neighbors asked the boys as they approached the party.

The mid-morning social was in full swing in our well-manicured park pavilion. The streets had been blocked off to allow us to interact and frolic safely. The neighbors were spirited and making merriment. The dads were tossing footballs and flying discs with the energetic young kids. The moms were arranging and serving up platters of food while sharing recipes and maybe even a bit of the latest, juicy, neighborhood gossip.

"Better hurry," Tom said to Bill. "Sally's devilled eggs are going fast. Hey, where the heck are Mary Ann and Hadley anyway?"

"Well, uh, it's funny that you should ask," Bill, said with an ashen face and a hint of panic in his voice. "We can't find Hadley.

"It's the craziest thing," he continued. "We were all in the house going about our business doing our chores, and she just seemed to have disappeared.

"She didn't happen to have come down here by any chance?" he asked eagerly.

"Why no, I haven't seen her. Hey, Sally," he called, "have you girls seen Hadley anywhere? They can't find her. She is not in the house."

"Oh my gosh!" Sally gasped as she registered the news. "You people have had more trouble than you deserve with that child!" She covered up her egg soufflé and jumped up on to the picnic table bench and yelled at the top of her lungs to quiet the jocular group.

"Everyone, quick, Hadley is missing!" she yelled. With an instinct of a heartfelt mother, she began to quickly organize kids and parents into small groups to search the streets. She instructed them to branch out in different directions to search for our missing child.

Bill ran down the street back to our house with Jack in tow and tears streaming down his face. He was overcome with gratitude for a bunch of neighbors who we barely knew, who apparently would be willing to drop everything in order to help us.

"Mary, any sign of her?" Bill asked anxiously as he reached the house.

"No!" I cried. "But, Bill, I called the police and they are on the way."

Our melancholic eyes locked for a brief moment and then we remembered that Jack was standing there with us. An unspoken understanding exchanged between us for a need to be strong in front of Jack. No sense worrying him, we thought. It was as though we had read each other's minds.

"Yes, Jack, your little sister is going to be just fine. We will find her," I said with conviction.

Two officers arrived and politely introduced themselves as they entered our home. We tried to remain calm as we frantically answered all of their questions.

"Yes, sir, we have lived here for five years," I answered factually.

"Yes, sir, we are married and these are both of our children."

"No, sir, we haven't had any marital issues of concern recently."

"Oh please, sir, can't we just continue to look for our baby?" I sobbed.

I repeated our activities of the morning and gave a detailed description of our daughter for the second time to the patient officers.

By now the whole neighborhood was buzzing with action, people were knocking on doors and yelling out Hadley's name. Some of these good neighbors even came into our home just to sit with us for support through this horrible inquisition.

"Let's just retrace all the steps," the female officer said as gently as she was trained to do.

The next half hour appeared to be freakishly surreal as we all re-enacted the activities of our morning. The house was filled with people by now. There was Bill, Jack, and myself, plus two officers and six trusted neighbors. After the re-enactment of the morning's activities, we all started to just search the house.

"Where on earth is Hadley? How could she have disappeared so quickly?" I lamented.

One of the officers checked the downstairs closets

while the female officer went upstairs. She went into all of the bedrooms one by one and started flipping the mattresses on all of the beds. While downstairs during the search, I even saw the other officer looking in our oven.

"The oven? Really?" I asked sarcastically.

"Ma'am, I've seen it all in the last twenty years, nothing surprises me," he said reproachfully.

One by one the different groups of searching neighbors came back to the house with the dismal news of having found neither hide nor hair of her.

I finally said to the officer, "I need to go up to Hadley's room one more time."

I slowly climbed the stairs and turned into her empty little room. I opened up her closet and got down on my knee's and prayed.

"Dear, God, please show us where Hadley is. Please bring her back to us," I pleaded.

I walked out of the closet, closed the door, and walked back into my room. And to my bewildered eyes, there she sat ever so sweetly, my baby, right on my bed! The mattress was still overturned. I screamed out her name so loudly that everyone in the house came running up the stairs and crammed into my bedroom.

I picked up my baby, who no one was able to find for the past two hours, and squeezed the daylights out of her! The whole room was sobbing, even the officers.

The female officer said, "This is unbelievable! We searched every inch of your house, ma'am! I even turned over the mattress that she is sitting on!"

The male officer reported that in all his years on the

beat, and just when he thought he had seen it all, this one truly took the cake!

A few nights later, mulling things over in my head about the horrific ordeal, I would continue to rack my brain.

Did I or didn't I lock the screen doors? I'm sure that I did, I must have.

But...then...did Hadley get out somehow and just wander around the yard and then somehow sneak back into the house?

But how did she get back up the stairs and into my room without being seen by anyone?

I would continue to ponder those questions for years. Whether Hadley had gotten out of the house that morning or not, it just seems eerily strange that two police officers, three family members, and six of the neighbors, all in the house searching for a little baby, couldn't seem to find her anywhere. She just suddenly appeared about as fast as she had disappeared!

There was never a dull moment for our big city neighbors while we resided in that wonderful residential community. It still touches our souls to this day that our entire group of friends would drop everything to lend a hand in our time of need. As for Hadley and her incredible disappearing magic trick, I guess we will never know this side of heaven where that sweet baby went.

In trying to communicate with her days later as to try to gain any information, we would desperately ask, "Where did you go, baby?"

She would only point and grunt noises that sounded like

"There, there."

And the wandering continued…

Six months later our family wanted to take a simple camping trip. It was time to get the kids out of the city and experience the wild open outdoors. We planned to do some swimming, a little body surfing, and perhaps even some hiking. At any rate, our kids up to this point in time were pretty citified and we wanted to expose them to the rugged outdoors. We had made the long trek to one of the most beautiful campgrounds in the state. It was well worth the long wait in line to register and enter the park, we thought, as we pulled our van into an exquisite spot nestled up along a sandy dune.

"This is great," Bill exclaimed as he strategically began planning where to assemble the tent, our makeshift home for the next week.

It felt wonderful to finally get out of the vehicle and stretch our tired, sore bones. The van was jam-packed full of all our camping gear and the food was somewhere on the bottom of the pile. I decided to get the kids out of their seatbelts and then I would begin to prepare some lunch for this hungry crew. Jack and Hadley immediately began to explore their rustic environment and began gathering leaves and sticks to build a fort.

Good, I thought. *They look creatively amused and occupied. Now is a good time to start unpacking and start unwrapping our sandwiches.*

"Hey, big boy," Bill called over to Jack. "Could you give me a hand with this tent?"

"Sure, Dad," I heard him reply. I smiled happily as I returned to the lunch preparation.

Next, in a matter of what seemed like five minutes later, I headed over to where Hadley was playing in order to give her a drink box. But she was gone! I walked a couple of feet over to Jack and Bill where they were pounding the tent stakes into the ground.

"Hey, guys, you're really doing a great job. Jack, you are such a big helper to Dad now," I complimented. "Here is Hadley's drink. Is she with you guys?" I asked.

"No, but she was just playing over there." Bill pointed over to the car.

Not seeing her, I walked over to the van and figured that she had crawled back in there to get her dolls.

Not there.

I walked back over to the pile of leaves where she and her brother had been earlier attempting a fort, but she wasn't there either. I ran over to the camp neighbors and asked as calmly as I could if they had seen a little girl with blonde hair by any chance.

"No," they replied as they stoked their fire pit. "But we will keep an eye out for her."

I ran back to Jack and Bill and yelled, "For the love of God, Hadley is gone! I don't see her anywhere."

"You mean to tell me that we've only been here for half an hour and we have lost sight of her?" Bill said angrily.

I ignored any connotation of an attack on me that he

might have been implying. Immediately we all began to frantically run around our surrounding area. We ran up and over the dune and yelled out her name.

"Hadley, where are you?"

By now the other campers could sense our problem and began to ask information in order to help out.

"What does she look like, ma'am?" they asked. "About how old is she?"

Once again in our lives we were struck with the conviction of the inherent goodness of people, strangers, willing to help others in their time of need. With too much time rapidly lapsing by and Bill and I beginning to truly panic, we asked a neighbor to drive back up to the registration office to call 911.

I couldn't believe that this was happening again! We vowed after the last event that we would never let her out of our sight. *This can't be good for my health*, I mused. *How much anxiety can the human body handle without causing some serious damage?* I thought. *Oh God, why am I such a bad parent? Why can't I keep track of my own child?*

The police officers had arrived to our campsite, and, once again, I was told to stay put with the female officer as we went over the routine questions. All I desperately wanted to do was bolt out of there and search for my child. Why couldn't she speak? Why didn't she have the ability to just tell me that she was going somewhere?

An hour had passed as Jack and I sat with the officer on the picnic table bench. I tried to keep Jack as calm as possible as we played crazy eights together. Kids of all ages were checking in and out of our campsite, on their bikes and roller blades, to see if Hadley had returned. The sound of the helicopter overhead caught my attention as I dreaded the thought that my baby could be anywhere near the water's edge!

"Oh my God!" I cried. "My poor baby can't even swim. No, no, it isn't possible that my baby, within an hour of us unpacking the van to set up camp, could have gone up and over the dune and headed toward the beach. Not Hadley." But another hour later that was exactly what we would be told.

It appeared that Hadley was able to climb up and over the rugged dune and found herself on the shore of the huge lake.

"She just seemed to be carelessly trundling along the beach," reported the young couple that was able to coax Hadley back to safety. "We thought, 'What a cute little girl, but what is a little girl doing out here all by herself? She must have walked at least a mile.'

"She was just walking along heading toward the lighthouse as if on a mission. When we saw the helicopter hovering above the lakeshore, we put two and two together," the couple explained.

While still holding Hadley, I embraced the young couple tightly. I thanked them profusely and I praised God that they, the couple that found her, were good, honest, decent people.

Three strikes and you're out!

Yes, there really was a third and final time that we would lose sight of our Hadley.

By now you are probably asking, "Whoever gave you the permission to have children?"

And trust me, I would be the first one to raise my hand and concur with your inquiry. *Lord,* I would lament, *there must be so many other people who are much more qualified to do this job than me.*

Hadley was still not able to speak, but we thought that we had every barrier in place to prevent any more tragic escapes. But Hadley, on our second day of arrival to our new small town, would once again be on the move.

We were all so exhausted from pushing and shoving all the boxes around the basement. There were so many boxes of stuff and way too many decisions to make right now in terms of where to put it all.

"The major furniture is in place, so let's just give it a rest for now. Besides, we have all summer to unpack it later," Bill said.

"Hey, Jack, the neighbor told me of a marina just down the block that we could go fishing in. I say we grab those new poles we bought and try our luck."

Jack happily agreed with Bill, as this would be his first time ever to be really going fishing. Looking around the neatly stacked boxes in the basement, I couldn't refuse their well-deserved request. I swooped up Hadley and laughed while telling her how silly I thought her daddy and brother would look being two city boys out there fishing for the first time.

"Gee, I hope they don't accidently throw those new poles in the lake while casting a line." I giggled. "For that would surely give us away that we are not from here."

Hadley, still not able to talk, giggled back as we headed up to the living room. My lovely baby seemed to understand me, yet she just couldn't seem to speak. My aching heart sighed.

"Hey, baby girl, lets you and I relax a bit ourselves. What story should we read?" I asked.

Instead of answering, Hadley just tugged one of her favorite books out of the pile on the coffee table.

"Clifford it is," I said, taking the small book from her hands. "Good choice sweetie." I smiled.

We were snuggled up in our comfy chair and on page 3 when the phone rang.

Holy cow, I thought, *I wonder who that could be. Who would be calling? We have only been here for two days.*

In a matter of five to six minutes that it took to deal with the business on the phone, I returned to the living room and once again Hadley was gone. I ran hysterically through the house, screaming and searching for Hadley.

Blast it all if that kid isn't faster than lightning! I thought.

I had promised myself that this would never happen again.

"Dear God, I really cannot take this anymore. Why don't you help me with this child? I need more help!" I scolded.

Convinced that Hadley was nowhere to be found in the

house, I started running around the yard.

"Hi, I'm your new neighbor." I waved to the bewildered looking face of the person across the fence. "We just moved in yesterday. We have an autistic child and right now I can't find her anywhere!" I rattled off a million miles per hour.

Oh my gosh! I thought. *What a great first impression of a crazy lady who couldn't keep track of her own kids,* I could imagine her thinking of me.

But to my surprise, the neighbor began to run in step with me, frantically darting about throughout the neighborhood.

"What is her name and how old is she? What does she look like?" she asked as she huffed and puffed to keep up with me.

Gasping from being winded and chocking down sobs, I answered all of her questions.

"Her name is Hadley. She is four and a half years old. She has large brown eyes and curly blonde hair but the biggest problem," I said, "is that she cannot speak. She cannot discern danger and I am afraid that she would go with any stranger if asked." I sobbed.

With no luck so far in the neighborhood, we headed back to the house. Bill and Jack had just returned and were about to tell of their great white whale tales when Bill sensed by the look on my face that we were in trouble again.

The police were called, and once again I found myself in the company of the female officer who insisted that I stay put here at home while the others continued to search for Hadley. I tried to explain to the best of my ability about the issues and problems of raising an autistic child.

"Autistic kids have issues with wandering," I tried to explain, as if attempting to make excuses and cover up for my own pitiful self.

My face grew hot with humiliation, upon confessing that this was in fact the third time that we had lost our daughter. The officer just sat calmly and appeared to be un-accusing as we gently swung back and forth on our porch swing.

Dear God, I am really losing it this time, I feared as my mind drifted somewhere very far away. My whole body felt numb and I felt what a sense of shock must feel like as it engulfs the human body and mind. I was already trying to prepare myself somehow for the possibility that Hadley might not ever come back to us.

Oh my God, is this really happening? She has been gone for over three hours. That is way too long for a sweet, helpless baby to be out on the street by herself. The loud screeching sounds of what sounded like hard-hitting brakes shook me back into reality.

Oh dear God, please protect my baby! Lord, she doesn't even know to stop and look both ways for cars.

Please send out all your angels today! I pleaded.

Once again, the word of a missing little girl on the loose, spread like wildfire around the neighborhood. People who we were meeting for the very first time were all out on foot searching and yelling out Hadley's name. One of the neighbors suggested that we call the local radio station in order to quickly alert the town of our dilemma. She avowed that the radio was the pipeline to communication for the community. But I was horrified by the suggestion. Coming from a large city that would be the last thing on earth that you would want to do. That would invite all kinds of possible unwanted trouble. But after a continuous flow of unsuccessful reports of her location, coming in to the officer on the porch, I was finally convinced to make that call in to the radio.

"Don't it make my brown eyes blue," Dori sang along with the radio as she washed the last plate from lunch at her sink. Opening up her kitchen window a bit farther to let in the warm spring air, she looked out over to her rose bushes.

I really need to add some lilacs to my garden this year, she thought.

Her eyes casually gazed around her yard as she planned her spring gardening when she spotted the sweet little girl. A little girl, happily swinging on the old, rusted swing set that her grandkids had abandoned years earlier.

"A little girl about five years old," the announcer from the radio had said. "Blonde hair and large brown eyes," he reported.

"'*Oh, how sad for the family*,' I thought when I had heard the interruption for the emergency alert on the afternoon program. Could this be…? That's…got to be…the little girl," Dori concluded. She dashed out to her yard.

"Hi, sweetie, what's your name?" she asked as she gently approached her.

"Hadley," said the little girl almost inaudibly.

"What a pretty name," Dori replied tenderly. "What's your last name, baby?"

"Hadley," repeated the sweet little girl with an infectious smile.

"Really, how interesting," said Dori.

Two years later singing at choir practice in my new church, my folder partner Dori, would remind me of that unfortunate afternoon.

"You don't remember me," she asked, "do you?"

"What do you mean?" I inquired with a puzzled look.

She retold the story of how she had found Hadley swinging so innocently in her yard that afternoon, and I was instantly thrust back into the nightmare. I'll never forget the female officer's words saying to me as we sat on the porch: "They believe a little girl was found that might fit the description of your daughter. They are heading over to the house right now."

The van pulled slowly into our drive, the side door slid open, and the two most beautiful hands that I had ever seen before in my life were steadily cradling my Hadley. I'll never forget that day or the sight of those strong hands that were holding my little girl. At first I could only look at the hands and then the little legs and feet that they were holding. I recognized those tiny, worn pink shoes. It was as if I was terrified to look at the face of the child for fear that it would not be that of my Hadley. But it was Hadley! And once again by the grace of God, and the small-town form of communication through a radio program, Hadley was brought back safe and sound.

I once was lost but now I'm found, was blind but now I see. And what amazing grace did we continue to receive.

The Church

In the very beginning stages of our hardship dealing with autism, there were few places where we could go that we considered safe. Our home, the school, and the church all comprised the list. I would like to share some stories about the church. The church itself, though the Word of God remains constant, can vary depending on the type of doctrine, music, and worship style that it provides. It can also exhibit an atmosphere with varying degrees of flexibility or rigidity.

It took us a while to find a fit for our family, especially with Hadley who was now seven years old. We needed all of the flexibility that we could find. We actually stayed out of church for a while because, well, let's just say it just hadn't work out for us. It would be a year after our move before we could muster the courage to seek out a house of worship. *It will work out this time*, we assured ourselves, as our knees quaked walking up the steps to the entrance. I had a death grip on Hadley's arm, weaving and bobbing through the crowded vestibule trying to be unnoticed. *Unnoticed. Yeah, that will happen before the second coming*, I sneered.

Coming new into any church in itself can be intimidating, but try coming in with a special child in a very small town. Remember, in the very beginning on this journey of autism, these special kids were scarcely understood by their own parents, much less the society at large. This church was ornate and adorned with large, colorful, stained glass windows. It had a musty smell that hinted at its age. We tried to make eye contact with a few friendly looking people but mostly kept our eyes low to the ground.

"This is just a trial period," I reminded our small, bungling group. "We will just hang back and observe things," I proclaimed.

"Tuck in your shirt, Jack," Bill instructed.

We were nervously shuffling in the hall among some latecomers rushing in to take their seats. Somewhat afraid to enter into the sanctuary, I suddenly spotted a long bench at the end of the hall where we awkwardly lingered. The music had just started and we needed to do something quick.

"The penalty bench," I quietly whispered, half joking at the bench's appearance. "Let's sit there"—I pointed—"and hurry before someone spots us."

After sitting there for a few minutes, I said self-assuredly, "There, this isn't so bad. We can hear everything being said without being seen."

That heavenly penalty bench would become our safety zone for the next three months. This ritual was actually working out. We would arrive just a few minutes before the service started. We would make brief pleasantries with attendees coming in late and then take to our bench for misfits. Jack often referred to it as the bench of shame, but heck, it was working for us. Hadley was free to roam back and forth as necessary. She could flap her wings and chirp like a bird out here all she wanted. No one could see or hear her, and yet we could hear the message being delivered. We rather enjoyed our personal secret haven until one morning an intruder interrupted it.

"Hello, you sweet little family," said the kind voice of a tall, stately looking woman. "Do you mind?" She scooted in onto the bench right between Hadley and me. "I've noticed that you all sit out here each Sunday morning." She gently started stroking Hadley's hair.

Oh dear, I gulped. I wondered if this sweet, soft-spoken woman had been voted by the Deacon Board to come out and give us the unfortunate news. *Oh well, I thought, we had made it a good three-month run this time.*

But much to our surprise, she just simply sat with us and continued to do so each week. She was always so kind to Hadley and would always pat and stoke her hair. Eventually the conversations moved beyond the condition of the weather. She introduced herself as Lois and was just content to unabashedly join our nonconforming entourage. As the weeks rolled on, Lois began asking more thoughtful questions about Hadley. It was as if she truly wanted to try to understand her. She reminded us each week of how had a death grip on Hadley's arm, weaving and bobbing through the crowded vestibule trying to be unnoticed. *Unnoticed. Yeah, that will happen before the second coming*, I sneered.

Coming new into any church in itself can be intimidating, but try coming in with a special child in a very small town. Remember, in the very beginning on this journey of autism, these special kids were scarcely understood by their own parents, much less the society at large. This church was ornate and adorned with large, colorful, stained glass windows. It had a musty smell that hinted at its age. We tried to make eye contact with a few friendly looking people but mostly kept our eyes low to the ground.

"This is just a trial period," I reminded our small, bungling group. "We will just hang back and observe things," I proclaimed.

"Tuck in your shirt, Jack," Bill instructed.

We were nervously shuffling in the hall among some latecomers rushing in to take their seats. Somewhat afraid to enter into the sanctuary, I suddenly spotted a long bench at the end of the hall where we awkwardly lingered. The music had just started and we needed to do something quick.

"The penalty bench," I quietly whispered, half joking at the bench's appearance. "Let's sit there"—I pointed—"and hurry before someone spots us."

After sitting there for a few minutes, I said self-assuredly, "There, this isn't so bad. We can hear everything being said without being seen."

That heavenly penalty bench would become our safety zone for the next three months. This ritual was actually working out. We would arrive just a few minutes before the service started. We would make brief pleasantries with attendees coming in late and then take to our bench for misfits. Jack often referred to it as the bench of shame, but heck, it was working for us. Hadley was free to roam back and forth as necessary. She could flap her wings and chirp like a bird out here all she wanted. No one could see or hear her, and yet we could hear the message being delivered. We rather enjoyed our personal secret haven until one morning an intruder interrupted it.

"Hello, you sweet little family," said the kind voice of a tall, stately looking woman. "Do you mind?" She scooted in onto the bench right between Hadley and me. "I've noticed that you all sit out here each Sunday morning." She gently started stroking Hadley's hair.

Oh dear, I gulped. I wondered if this sweet, soft-spoken woman had been voted by the Deacon Board to come out and give us the unfortunate news. *Oh well, I thought, we had made it a good three-month run this time.*

But much to our surprise, she just simply sat with us and continued to do so each week. She was always so kind to Hadley and would always pat and stoke her hair. Eventually the conversations moved beyond the condition of the weather. She introduced herself as Lois and was just content to unabashedly join our nonconforming entourage. As the weeks rolled on, Lois began asking more thoughtful questions about Hadley. It was as if she truly wanted to try to understand her. She reminded us each week of how beautiful our daughter was and, oh, what gorgeous hair, she would declare.

Over the next three months, Lois melted our hearts with her kindness. It wasn't pity that was bestowed upon us but rather a genuine acceptance of us.

Because of her we would eventually take the leap of faith and enter through the tall wooden doors of the sanctuary.

It was now two years later and a long time since we'd given any thought to the bench of shame. We now attended the church each week, arriving bright and early, confidently walking in sprightly along with the others.

"Good morning, Mrs. Smith, you're sure looking good this morning," I said.

"Why, thank you. I read about Hadley in the paper yesterday. What a nice job she did in the talent show. Why I had no idea what a beautiful little voice she has," she replied.

Thanks to our dear Lois, people in the church had been informed of our family's struggles regarding our special needs child. Any fears that some may have had all seemed to have vanished. We were now making friends and being invited to all kinds of fun and social activities. It seemed that once the autism was explained and some suggested methods for possible trouble-shooting were given, Hadley was welcomed and well received by all. Everyone appeared to be quite taken with her.

"Oh, she says the funniest things," Sara, the Sunday school teacher, chortled. "And wasn't that hilarious last week when pastor was preaching, Remember? Right in the middle of his sermon, when he rhetorically asked, 'And so, do you really believe?' he asked with a slight intentional pause for effect, and then Hadley, without missing a beat, responded with a loud, 'Yes!'

"It cracked me up to see how our sleepy congregation erupted into uncontrollable laughter," she chuckled, "as we all watched our beloved pastor try to collect himself."

Now that the church families' fears of the unknown had been addressed and defused, our family could begin to relax a bit. I was beginning to feel so comfortable that I even decided that I should join the choir. It had been way too long since I had the chance to participate and, oh, how I love to sing. After all, I don't really need to sit with Hadley every week. Besides, she could sit in the pew confined between her dad and brother while I sang up in the loft with all of the others. What could possibly go wrong?

It was all going smoothly until that one fateful morning when a rigid Sunday service turned saintly wild. The new choir director had been bringing in new livelier music each week. We all loved it and had a lot of fun learning it. Oh, how the congregation would feel the spirit move on this new tune, he prided himself. As we were practicing one night, joyously singing to high heaven, a scary thought occurred to me as my mind momentarily drifted from my musical score.

I had a sudden vision that made my hair stand on end.

No, she wouldn't dare! I let out a panicked breath. Just because this music happens to be extremely rhythmic and bouncy doesn't automatically mean that Hadley would react. *She exhibits so much more control these days*, I thought reproachfully. *Don't be silly.* I promptly filed that annoying thought to the back recesses of my mind and turned my attention back to my music.

Music can be a very spiritual, heartfelt part of worship. This was the morning that the choir was going to help make that happen for the congregation. We had been practicing for weeks on our new song. This song was very different from any kind of songs that we had performed. This song of worship was very lively and jazzy, yet had a very tropical feel to it. It had blaring horns blowing while rhythmic bongos kept the beat. And sure enough, that morning the choir proved to be successfully delivering, as people appeared to be pleasantly surprised. Their hands and feet were moving to the beat as they gave each other nods of approval.

The choir was swaying as one as we sang with gusto to the spiritual tropical tune. We were singing like we had never sung before. It was a new and refreshing song, and we were all feeling the spirit move. Oh, how pleased was the look on the choir director's face. His expressions were quite animated as he directed us, his arms flailed wildly in time.

"Don't... you want.... to be.... a part... of the kingdom?" He mouthed the lyrics in syncopation with his accommodating choir.

"Oh, this is going to be great," he whispered to us under

his breath in between the verses. "And to think that I've only been here for two weeks."

What a joyous sound the choir was lending to the congregation. The melodic fervor seemed to permeate all the way up to heaven. I knew the song well enough and we were really going strong. I decided to take a peep above my music folder. I wanted to see for myself how the flock was receiving us and also to make double sure that all was well with my Hadley. From scanning the congregation, I could see that most of them seemed to be experiencing shear spiritual delight. I even noticed that the pastor was tapping his foot, keeping time, and smiling from ear to ear.

Oh, to be singing again. How great to be a part of something so wonderful. Thank you, God, for church choir and Sunday mornings, I thought wistfully.

That's when I saw the little girl. I saw a little girl bearing a strong resemblance to my Hadley and wearing a "Cheshire cat's" grin. This little girl was flapping her wings to beat the band and heading right up the center aisle.

"Oh dear God!" I gasped. "She *is* really going to do it!" That horrid thought that I had during practice was coming true.

Hadley had a really hard time controlling her impulses, especially where music was involved. She probably had contained herself for as long as she possibly could but just couldn't help herself any longer. She had to cut loose and move to the groove. The music was just that contagious.

Trying to stay calm and not lose my focus on my singing, I scanned the pews for Bill. Surely, he would do something. "What the heck?" my eyes translated when they launched like missiles into his. "Do something," my eyes pleaded. Bill just helplessly sat there, still as a statue, and shrugged his shoulders as he sunk deep into the pew.

Unaware of all the commotion that was rippling throughout the place, the director was oblivious to all of the pandemonium going on behind him. What a scene it was. He continued, with eyes focused on the choir, fiercely conducting his way to fame without a clue as to what was going on behind him. By now Hadley had reached her destination and was dancing in full swing. There she was dancing right upon the altar. She was smack dab behind the unsuspecting director. Gasps from the audience went from snickers to full-blown, yet stifled, laughter.

As I watched in horror, I thought to myself, *You know that kid really has some pretty good moves. Stop it! I scolded myself. What are you thinking? This isn't funny. Remember where you are. You are in a church!*

Never suspecting a thing, the director was doing a dance of another kind.

My job is secure, he mused to himself. *This song is great and they love me. Why else would all of that wild commotion be going on behind me?* he enthused, still facing the choir. *I've never witnessed my choir so alive*, he thought as he moved and swayed.

The gleeful faces beaming from the choir members only seemed to further his enthusiasm. Just then my folder partner jabbed me in the ribs and chortled, "Hey, isn't that your daughter?"

"Daughter," I replied mortified. "What daughter? I've never seen that girl before in my life."

I held my head high and continued singing. Mercifully after what seemed to be an eternity of hilarious calamity, Maria, a trusted girlfriend sitting out in the pews approached the altar. She mustered the gumption to bravely approach Hadley and was successfully able to convince her to end her performance. She gently took Hadley by the hand and directed her back to her seat. By now this house of worship was up for grabs. People were trying their best to conceal their fits of laughter and knee slapping.

The director was beside himself with his obvious incredible performance, not suspecting for a moment that there were two shows going on that Sunday morning. The song finally ended as he wiped the bit of perspiration from his brow. The director turned from us and bowed to his adoring audience. The entire church body leaped to their feet and gave a thunderous applause.

"Oh, I don't know when I've had more fun in church," Mrs. McCrath cried as she wiped her eyes and straightened her turquoise hat.

Well, I thought, for sure this time we will be receiving our letter of dismissal from the Deacon Board in the mail this week. Hadley had surely broken all the rules, this time by *dancing* in the church.

But like King David, that beautiful, unpretentious child danced freely with all her might. Somehow I really didn't think that God had minded. God has a sense of humor and obviously so did the members of our great church family. We never did receive that letter. If laughter is good medicine, as the proverb tells us, then Hadley healed a lot of souls that morning.

Hadley, in her unassuming and direct innocence, continued to touch many lives in our church.

Often an unfamiliar face would approach me and declare, "Oh, you must be Hadley's mom. I just want to tell you that your daughter has greeted us on several occasions here at the church. You see we are new here and haven't met a lot of people, but your daughter, Hadley, comes over to us each week. She marched right up to us and said, 'Hi, I'm Hadley Rose Payne. Who are you?'

"'Why, I am Kate and this is my husband, Tom,' I replied. 'Oh.' She giggled. 'I would like to be your friend, and, by the way, you look like Glenda and he looks like the scarecrow from *The Wizard of Oz*.' Then she did a twirl around us and still giggling said, 'Bye.'"

How could a church know that they would be getting a built-in greeter and one that lends "character" as well? That's our Agent H; we would begin to refer to her at home as one of God's best ambassadors. We were really beginning to see the hope for Hadley and the healing for the rest of us.

Many years later, Hadley would be invited to join the choir.

"She sings so beautifully and right on pitch. She is such a blessing to us all," exclaimed the director. That week our Pastor Carlson invited Hadley to join the choir. One of Hadley's beloved friends agreed to be her folder partner.

Each week Corey would help her read the notes so she could sing along with the rest of the choir. Corey had such a calming affect and genuine love for her. Because of that friendship, we were able to sit comfortably in our seats without having anxiety as we listened to them each week. Corey was so fond of Hadley that they not only became chums but also eventually even sang duets together for an offertory, twice to a standing ovation.

"You make beautiful things, out of the dust. You make beautiful things out of us."[2]

The two sweet girls sang together in front of a packed church. What a beautiful song they sang and how appropriate the lyrics. The congregation stood for five minutes, clapping and wiping their eyes.

No matter what kind of people we are, there is much to be learned from each other. To this day our Hadley continues to begin each and every one of her prayers with the words "Great God and Heavenly Father"—a prayer that Hadley had audibly learned from hearing it being said week after week by our beloved Pastor Carlson. Just when you think that she isn't paying any attention, she is actually absorbing like a little sponge.

Let the children come to me. Don't stop them! For the Kingdom of Heaven belongs to those who are like these children.

Matthew 19:14

The School

It was one of the hottest days in late May that I could remember. There we sat like sardines in that over-packed gymnasium on graduation day for the class of 2010.

Mrs. Tulak tapped my shoulder from behind.

"Isn't this exciting?" she squealed. "Our babies are graduating!"

"I know," I said while wiping the perspiration from my brow. "It seems like only yesterday we were braiding their hair and walking them to the bus."

"You must be so proud of your Hadley," she said sincerely. "And to think that she made it all the way to senior year."

"It is a bit hard to believe," I concurred with tears developing in my eyes.

I turned my attention back to the platform as the band began to play Pomp and Circumstance.

You could feel the exhilaration in the airless gym.

Student after student took to the stage to receive their diploma.

Oh dear God, I thought. *Where is she?*

I could barely handle the anxiety. How was my baby doing with all of the anticipation? The ceremony seemed to drone on and on. There were over a hundred students in the class. Would Hadley wait patiently for her turn? Students and family members were screaming and yelling out for students as they strutted across the platform.

"Way to go Alex!"

"Whoo hoo, Jessica! You did it!"

Oh dear, I stressed. *Will there be dead silence when Hadley walks across?*

I finally spotted Hadley, dead last in line.

An eternity had passed and it was finally her turn. She was at the bottom of the steps, only three students away from her ascent. My heart was pounding louder than the drums in the band. With palms sweating and with glazed eyes, I turned to Bill and Jack.

"Okay, guys," I said to my little family. "Here comes Hadley. No matter what other people think or who stares at us, let's scream like there is no tomorrow for her.

"Here she comes," I cried. "On the count of three. "One, just close your eyes," I said. "Two, get ready."

Before I could count to three, as we opened our mouths to yell out, we were joined by a thunderous noise. We heard screaming, yelling, and clapping by the entire student body for our baby girl. There they were, all on their feet, hooting and hollering for our Hadley. We fell back into our seats sobbing.

Hadley truly was loved and accepted by this incredible group of classmates. It took us about twenty minutes to compose ourselves.

Later, while having coffee and cake with other parents, I couldn't help but reflect back on how it all had begun…

The last box had been emptied out and the furniture had been arranged promptly in our new home. It was the middle of August and classes would resume within two weeks. The next thing on the list of things to do was to take the kids over to the new school and sign them up.

"Nice to meet you, and welcome to our community," said the awaiting principal cheerfully.

We shuffled into the quaint elementary school building as the friendly administrator said, "So I understand that your daughter is autistic?"

"Yes," I answered weakly and with some trepidation.

"So I finally get to meet you, Hadley." She winked at us as she reached out a hand to her. "I read all about you in the paper last month. Just glad that it all worked out for you folks and that she was found safe and sound," she said sincerely.

"And to think, remembering back while reading the paper about a missing little girl, I said to myself, 'This one's coming to *my* school.'

"Well, I am here to inform you," continued the dignified principal, "that I believe that Hadley will do just fine here in our school."

Then she went on to explain that the school district offered "inclusion" and that every child, including children with learning disabilities, has the right to participate.

We brushed away the tears gathering in our eyes as we considered her unbelievable words. Obediently we followed in step with the principal as we toured our new revealed gem of a school.

The small community that we found ourselves living in allowed Hadley to participate in the regular education program. This was one of the main reasons for the move as this concept was unheard of where we had come from. The school not only admitted her to the inclusion of regular education but also even provided a full-time aide to help provide instruction.

This aide turned out to be an angel dressed in human clothing as she profoundly touched Hadley's life. Jan had the patience of Job and then some. She worked patiently with Hadley from kindergarten until one year after graduation. Jan spent about the same amount of time with Hadley as I did, if not more throughout the school year.

She had the arduous task of working with Hadley during the beginning, middle, and final stages of her dietary treatment program. And in the beginning, it was quite a chore. In order for Hadley to exhibit the full benefits of the treatment program regarding her behavior, Hadley had to follow a rigid diet. It took months for her body to fully absorb the vitamins and nutrients we were adding to her system. In the interim, she was not yet processing information very well and was quite unruly at times. If she strayed at all from the steady course of gluten/dairy-free foods, her actions could change on a dime. But Hadley cheated a lot, even though the physical pain cost her dearly. In the early days of Hadley's treatment, poor Jan chased that child all around that school. But the school and the aide never gave up on trying to teach Hadley the concepts of appropriate behavior.

The school was always trying new and innovative techniques in order to help Hadley. In elementary school, Hadley's academic performance was monitored all day long based on a point system. The idea was to improve and increase appropriate conduct. Check marks were charted and posted on a board used to point out negative practices that needed to be changed. If more than three check marks were accrued that week, the consequences resulted in privileges being taken away. The goal was to receive no check marks. To see those check marks by your name was a bad thing. Even Hadley seemed to understand the concept of the dreaded check mark. Yet she had already accrued three for the week. But the elimination of privileges was settled at the end of the week.

One day during that same week, Hadley had a pretty good morning as she was following directions and making great attempts to do well.

"Hadley has managed herself quite well today, even she seems to be proud of herself," remarked the aide.

"She must not have tried to sneak into her brother's candy again," continued the aide to the teacher in the room. "She is so calm today. I think she is really trying hard to stick to the foods that she can eat, what a difference it makes in her," she boasted of her charge.

"I think I'll give her a great big shiny star to reward and encourage her. Oh, Hadley, I knew you could do it," rejoiced the aide.

Then Jan told Hadley that as a reward she could put the shiny star anywhere on the board that she wanted to. She figured Hadley would put it on her recently displayed artwork out in the hall. Maybe she would even place it on the collar of her pretty new red dress.

But, oh no, Hadley was much too clever to let this opportunity slip by. Wouldn't you know that our child, who didn't seem to understand math, science, or basic reasoning, went right over and promptly placed that great big star on the performance chart to cover up her third check mark?

That takes care of that, Hadley's impish grin implied. *Now no one will see the third check mark at the end of the week. Nothing to be taken away from me this week*, her giggled implied.

Oh, how Jan had to laugh herself at Hadley's quick wit. Just when you think she was not paying attention to detail. Outwitted again by Agent H.

Because of that Jan's genuine love, perseverance, and sense of humor, Hadley not only developed the meaning of a true friendship but also eventually learned to read and write as well. I am sure that Jan has enough stories regarding Hadley to write a book of her own someday. When Jan first started working with her, Hadley could barely talk. Years later, lovingly, the challenge would be to make her stop, but only for inappropriate situations.

The school district in our small town turned out to be an absolute blessing for our special child, it was above and beyond our comprehension. I cannot say enough about the teachers. They bestowed such kindness and patience upon Hadley and truly made her a part of their classes. I believe that the teachers are woven into the fabric of Hadley's heart as not a day goes by where she doesn't mention at least one of them.

One teacher in particular, Mrs. Nordine, from third grade, remembered how much Hadley had enjoyed reading her personal copy of *Disney's Treasury of Children's Classics*. She often read it to her students and it was one of Hadley's favorites. It was tucked away on a shelf in her classroom for years. Nine years later she signed it "With love" and gave it to Hadley at graduation.

Many of these teachers spent their personal time with Hadley during after-school hours, allowing her to play with their own children. There were times when Hadley was invited to family summer outings at their homes. Other times Hadley would be picked up to do one of her favorite things and that was to take a swing through McDonald's drive in for French fries.

It was incredible to think that teachers, during the summer months, would even consider the welfare of a student's loneliness. The teachers profoundly enriched Hadley's life. And not just them, everyone in the school system from the lunch aide to the superintendent befriended Hadley and benefitted from her life.

I remember one bus driver telling me a few years later of his fears of having a special needs child on the bus. And then after getting to know Hadley, he pronounced that Hadley was considered to be one of his best buddies. "Oh, how she would laugh when I would yell to the other kids on the bus to sit down or be quiet," the driver said. "She would laugh so hard, mocking and imitating me so well that the other kids were entertained by her reaction. It was like they were shocked right back into their seats. They would instantly knock off all their commotion. I loved having that kid on my bus."

I'll never forget the day, while shopping at the local grocer; when another school bus driver, named Charlie approached me.

"I have to tell you Mrs. Payne, said the charming mature gentleman, Hadley has blessed me many a day while driving her to school."

"Oh?"

"I have been picking her up each morning for the past five years. But there was that one day, he began, I was just going about my business driving that old familiar route from your house to the middle school.

Well sometimes, he continued, I'd just get to whistling, an old habit of mine. I would just drive and whistle and drop off one kid at a time. Hadley was the last one on the scheduled route and I have to admire how patiently she sat and waited her turn. I looked up in the rear-view mirror as I often did and there was Hadley just a smiling. That smile could melt an iceberg."

"We're almost there kiddo," I assured her, looking back at her through the rear view mirror, and then I went back to my mindless whistling.

As I whistled, I began to hear another sound on the bus. It was the sweetest sound that you ever heard, almost like the sound of an angel. I looked again in the rear view mirror and I realized that it was Hadley singing. She was accompanying me with words to the song Amazing Grace that I was whistling to."

I listened to this kind man tell his story as I brushed back the tears from my eyes.

"She sang out softly, he went on, each and every verse, throwing in a couple of her own words and phrases cuz I guess she didn't know the exact words."

"Yes indeed, he continued, I do believe that that was the sweetest thing that ever touched my soul," he proclaimed.

Imagine, I thought to myself as this man told me his Hadley story, a child who keeps to herself for the most part, never talks to anyone on the bus, connected with an old bus driver in such a powerful way by taking an ordinary day and making it extraordinary. You never know when you may be entertaining angels.

> I will praise God's name by singing to him. I will bring him glory by giving him thanks.
>
> *Psalms 69:30*

Another time it was a simple phone call from a janitor during the first week of summer vacation. We were so excited to be starting our lovely three months of freedom and relaxation. While rearranging closets for summer wear, I discovered that Hadley's prescription glasses were missing. For two days, we retraced our steps along the sidewalks to and from town.

"Let's check the library," I said, since we had just been there two days prior. Without luck we checked all of our familiar spots around town. *If we could only find them*, I lamented. They were so expensive and we had just purchased them a few months ago.

Oh, if only I were a better mother and could keep better track of things, I scolded myself. I still tended to make little things so big.

Oh well, I guess we will just go back to the doctor this week and buy another pair, I thought.

Later that night, while eating popcorn and watching *The Lion King* with the kids, the phone rang.

"Hi, Mrs. Payne," said the recognizable soft tone of the janitor. "Say, is Hadley missing a pair of glasses by any chance?"

"Yes," I gratefully sang into the phone.

drop off one kid at a time. Hadley was the last one on the scheduled route and I have to admire how patiently she sat and waited her turn. I looked up in the rear-view mirror as I often did and there was Hadley just a smiling. That smile could melt an iceberg."

"We're almost there kiddo," I assured her, looking back at her through the rear view mirror, and then I went back to my mindless whistling.

As I whistled, I began to hear another sound on the bus. It was the sweetest sound that you ever heard, almost like the sound of an angel. I looked again in the rear view mirror and I realized that it was Hadley singing. She was accompanying me with words to the song Amazing Grace that I was whistling to."

I listened to this kind man tell his story as I brushed back the tears from my eyes.

"She sang out softly, he went on, each and every verse, throwing in a couple of her own words and phrases cuz I guess she didn't know the exact words."

"Yes indeed, he continued, I do believe that that was the sweetest thing that ever touched my soul," he proclaimed.

Imagine, I thought to myself as this man told me his Hadley story, a child who keeps to herself for the most part, never talks to anyone on the bus, connected with an old bus driver in such a powerful way by taking an ordinary day and making it extraordinary. You never know when you may be entertaining angels.

I will praise God's name by singing to him. I will bring him glory by giving him thanks.

Psalms 69:30

Another time it was a simple phone call from a janitor during the first week of summer vacation. We were so excited to be starting our lovely three months of freedom and relaxation. While rearranging closets for summer wear, I discovered that Hadley's prescription glasses were missing. For two days, we retraced our steps along the sidewalks to and from town.

"Let's check the library," I said, since we had just been there two days prior. Without luck we checked all of our familiar spots around town. *If we could only find them*, I lamented. They were so expensive and we had just purchased them a few months ago.

Oh, if only I were a better mother and could keep better track of things, I scolded myself. I still tended to make little things so big.

Oh well, I guess we will just go back to the doctor this week and buy another pair, I thought.

Later that night, while eating popcorn and watching *The Lion King* with the kids, the phone rang.

"Hi, Mrs. Payne," said the recognizable soft tone of the janitor. "Say, is Hadley missing a pair of glasses by any chance?"

"Yes," I gratefully sang into the phone.

Only in a small town could this ever have been possible. Where else would it happen that a night-time janitor, while going about his duties, would take the time to pick up a pair glasses and actually know who they belonged to and call the mother to claim them? I am here to tell you the answer is nowhere, except for my small town, where people know and care about each other.

Hadley's participation in regular education, aside from the academics, also allowed her to experience social peer interaction with other children. What these other children were not aware of at the time was that they were becoming significant role models in Hadley's life. They were living examples of normal friends for a thirsty, abnormal little girl ready to drink in all that she could. They were angels from heaven wrapped up in human clothing that bestowed upon Hadley unique love and acceptance. They took pride in mothering and nurturing her. For some it became cool to be Hadley's friend. For others it was as normal as any other ordinary friendship.

I remember one event that Hadley would participate in at Christmas time. She would be under the direction of a substitute teacher for a play. This teacher was not familiar with our Hadley. The teacher admitted to the fact that she was a bit nervous not having had a lot of experience with autistic kids.

"Oh dear," fretted the teacher, "how will I get her to do

the right things at the right time?" she sighed aloud.

"Not to worry," said Jimmy, one of Hadley's elementary classmates. He proudly stepped forward to the stage. "I know Hadley. I will take care of her," he beamed.

This young boy had been taught about autism in his classroom and felt that he understood Hadley enough to look out for her. To this day that teacher cannot tell that story without tears in her eyes. She was so moved by the compassion from someone so young regarding the outcome of another much less fortunate than he. Either directly or indirectly, Hadley seemed to affect others in such a unique way. Someday in heaven, I just know that there will be hundreds of people lined up who will tell me their Hadley stories.

There was another angel who is referred to as "my beloved" by Hadley. I believe that she has some jewels set aside for her crown in Heaven.

Emily was a sister, a friend, and a very beautiful, popular girl. A girl who certainly didn't have to spend her days with a special needs girl. She made a huge impact on Hadley's life. Emily was so comfortable in her own skin that she could actually make friends with an autistic person. She absolutely enjoyed spending time with Hadley. Because of her, Hadley got to partake in normal activities through out the school year. Hadley was able to play the drums in a pep band before basketball games. She got to hang out in coffee clubs with cute boys and pretty girls playing their guitars and socializing.

There were many times when Emily would arrange for several girls from the class to come over to the house and watch Disney movies with Hadley. But the birthday parties were the best. Her classmates would come over dressed up in costumes. Hadley loved to assign Disney characters to the girls and they were based on appearance and personality. The roaring noise level of laughter and squealing of elation was ear-splitting.

"Lets make this an annual event," one of the girls cried. "Even after we've gone off to college and are home on break," another one said.

"With Hadley, we will always remain young," they all agreed.

Emily shared her graduation open house celebration with Hadley allowing her to experience an amazing last hurrah with all of their classmates. Emily has told me on numerous occasions, "Oh no, Mrs. Payne, you don't need to thank me for spending time with Hadley. I thank *you*. You don't know how much I love to be with her and what she does for me. I truly consider her to be one of my best friends!"

If education is the process of teaching and acquiring information then truly everybody has learned something by including Hadley, our agent H.

Oh my people, listen to my teaching. Open your ears to what I am saying.

Psalms 78:1

MARY ANN PAYNE, M. A.

May 27, 2010

Dear Hadley,

As we started other friendship and adventures, twelve years ago, you have changed from a cute "Little Pixie" to a beautiful "Princess."

There have been laughs and cries, happy and sad times, work and fun. But you have truly been a shining star not only in my eyes but truly in God's.

He has and will always enlighten your life and give you his special Blessings now and forever.

Thank you for letting me be part of your life, I have treasured this time and will never forget the wonderful times we have shared and will have as we continue our friendship together though life.

Keep up your good work, Hadley. You can surly show others the true meaning of Love. You have a heart of gold that is rich in kindness, caring, and laughter.

Love always,

Jan

The Office Visit

The heated controversy over what causes autism and the method in which to treat it has created a boiling pot of alpha-bit soup stirring up physicians, Insurance companies and parents.

Because we chose to step out side of the American Medical Association's box re: reason for cause and treatment of autism we found ourselves frustrated on numerous occasions. Nonetheless, it all took place in the office.

The Treatment

One of the biggest obstacles in obtaining treatment for Hadley's autism was getting the coverage to actually pay for it. The procedures and protocols that we used were seen as radical and were not covered by our premiums. Our insurance company had their medical terms for treatment but they did not agree with ours. We chose to utilize alternative methods. Alternative means using biological rather than pharmacological methods.[3] The doctors that we had been taking Hadley to when she was an infant were within the traditional medical model. They offered only prescribed synthetic psychotropic medications. Those doctors offered a long list of drugs that they believed would have been of benefit to Hadley in order to treat her autism.

Bill and I were skeptical of the drugs. Our insurance company would have covered the drugs. However, the research that I had done on these medications and drugs, proved to have had possible, undesirable side effects. These side effects posed to cause even *greater* issues without even getting to the root of Hadley's problems. We believed that these medications would only mask her symptoms and not address the actual cause of her autism.

We found ourselves on a search for alternative treatment programs and physicians who could administer them. In 1999 Hadley was eight years old and we were introduced to a treatment approach called the Biomedical Assessment Options for children with Autism and Related Problems.

This assessment offered a unique protocol that was a result of a consensus report of a group called Defeat Autism Now! (DAN).[3] Though it was not a recommendation of diagnostic tests or treatment, the more we learned about the protocol, the more it made sense for us.

This protocol enabled us to take a look at Hadley as a

unique individual. It helped us to identify many of *her* physical problems and how they related to *her* autism. This program offered biomedical treatment options for her biochemical and immunological problems.[3] We started by taking a complete blood count, urinalysis, serum ferritin, and amino acid screen tests to list a few. It was the first time that her biochemistry was ever considered as being part of the solution for the healing process to begin. The results of these tests allowed us to look at the problems that we found and treat them accordingly.

More commonly, the tests allowed us to take a glance at Hadley's insides, conveying where *her* problems lie. Not every child with autism has the same biochemical makeup as we are all uniquely designed. So using a one size-fits-all solution treatment plan to cure, (psychotropic medication), just did not make sense to us.

The analysis of these tests also identified any presence of toxins and heavy metals found. These tests outlined the route we knew that we must take to bring about improvement for our daughter. These tests verified that Hadley not only had very high amounts of heavy metals and toxins in her blood system, but that she was also quite deficient in vitamin B6, vitamin D, magnesium, calcium, and zinc, as well as several other minerals. Once we discovered the underlying biochemical problems, we were able to begin treatment. Through extensive application of biomedical tests and treatments, our map was drawn. We discovered that with little to no side effects, Hadley could be treated with natural supplements to combat her deficiencies. We also discovered that Hadley could not digest and absorb foods containing gluten and casein. We began a diet of eliminating those foods. Also by adding the deficient vitamins and minerals back into her diet, we were able to reduce some of her problems that hampered her social behavior. We began to see dramatic improvement.

So for us the long list of medications that had previously been offered by conventional medicine had become inconsequential. Our insurance company would have covered them but we didn't want them. Somewhere down the road, whether by environment, vaccinations, genetics, or a combination of all of the above, Hadley was stripped of all the nutrients needed to make her body and mind function the way it was supposed to. Within months of administering this new treatment plan for Hadley, we started to see amazing results. We were on the road to recovery for our baby. There was just no insurance to cover it. Having said all of that, you may now begin to understand our predicament while at the office.

I would have thought that the world would have been rejoicing with us. We had searched to the ends of the earth and discovered the fountain of healing for our autistic child. Her healing and road to recovery had begun. It all made such perfect sense to us. We found the treatment protocol. We found the doctors to administer it. The patient was getting better. She was beginning to talk and make eye contact; she no longer walked on her toes and flapped her wings. I said to myself, *Just pay for the treatment so that we can all go home and thank you very much.*

But the insurance company did not believe or accept our claims. They were not allowed to play ball with us.

They would not cover any expenses incurred under such protocol. The doctors that applied these protocols were not in our insurance network. The protocol, even though it was working for our daughter, hadn't been approved by the American Medical Association, we were told. It was such shocking news from them, but we would not let it deter us because we were seeing improvement like never before. How could we stop this extraordinary progress, we sighed, as we reached deeper and deeper into our pockets?

Believe it or not, the treatment was simple food substitution, along with the chelating (removal) of the heavy toxins that were built up in her body, and the administration of natural vitamins and supplements. We didn't use any out-of-the-ordinary treatments or risky drugs. It was food substitution and natural, not harmful, supplements. There were no side effects from the application of any of these treatment methods.

Unfortunately the protocol was just simply outside of the traditional medical model. It was almost too good to be true. Hadley was improving and getting healthy. She was laughing and talking with her peers for the first time. She was beginning to read and take interest in a variety of new things. The only adverse side effect of the treatment that I could note was that my insurance company refused to pay for any of the special foods, the supplements, the chelation, and the doctor visits.

The financial part of treatment for some can really be a deterring factor. I remember the first time I had a meeting with all the local moms of kids on the autism spectrum in my community. I explained how effective the protocol was and how much improvement we were seeing in our daughter. I suggested that maybe by exploring or even applying this protocol they could get similar results with their own children. It certainly would be worth investigating. I thought that they would run me over to get in line to see about getting started. Instead they just sat there, staring at me as if I had three eyes and four arms. Later I discovered that it wasn't so much the approach or the protocol that stopped them, it was the price. The actual cost to carry out such a plan is exorbitant. And at that time there was no insurance coverage for the treatment.

As if the cruelty of autism itself wasn't enough to suck the life out of you, now, when finally we were getting treatment and progress, the medical world, along with the insurance companies, were there to knock you down again. It was as if they didn't want us to recover. They certainly didn't want to help pay. I guess if you have to pay for it, you have to name it. The naming of this disorder is one of the biggest controversies since the chicken and the egg. No one seems to want to talk about it except for those of us perplexed parents. One could clearly observe the progress in my child. She was focused, she was talking, and she was developing a sweet personality. So basically, I pay fifteen grand a year for health care and my insurance company won't pay my bills. My daughter is vastly improving and the traditional medical model won't condone her treatment. I just don't *get it*, (the coverage) literally!

Yes, just another day at the office… Insurance coverage or not, the treatment was working so we forged ahead.

Looking back thirteen years ago we were so ecstatic to

have finally discovered a real treatment plan to administer to Hadley in order to begin the healing process.

For the record this treatment plan was expensive and not easy to apply. Talk about blood, sweat and tears! So much for drama/trauma bestowed upon a little girls life. A little girl who couldn't tell her mommy what hurt her but instead just coped and endured the pain as though it were all a part of her abnormal life. A little girl who couldn't understand any kind of reasoning or explanation of such necessary procedures to improve the quality of her life but just complied.

Bill and I were incredibly overwhelmed. These were very difficult years for our little family. These procedures required Hadley to undergo a series of blood draws, needle sticks, and the collection of urine and stool samples. Then there were the pills or supplements that had to be swallowed. She had to swallow dozens of pills each and every day. The pills looked to be the size of horse pills. A morning routine around the 'House of Payne' would be one of chasing that poor child from one end to the other to get her to try to swallow them.

What an aerobic workout we got throughout those years chasing and climbing, over and under every thing and anything to get to her. She had to swallow those pills and supplements in order for the nutritional remedy to take effect. Why couldn't there be a magic wand that we could just wave over her? Hadley would just run and scream with her hands over her mouth and yell, "No pills, No pills!"

We even tried to trick her at times by hiding the dreaded pills in a glob of pudding on a spoon.

"Look what I have Hadley," her brother Jack would coax. "Come and have some yummy chocolate pudding."

"Rats!" he sighed sulking back into the kitchen with the empty spoon. The spoon that had been expertly licked off of its creamy confection devoured by a very crafty child and leaving that dreaded pill sitting right there upon it.

We didn't think we would ever get through those exasperating years. But by the grace of God we did.

Then there were the doctors that we entrusted her care to. None of them practiced in our rural area. They were all three to four hours away from where we lived. We had to endure many days and nights of traveling in inclement weather not to mention the hundreds of dollars that we had to spend on gas to get there. So much time, effort and energy spent on simply going to and from the doctor's office. We were beginning to doubt our move away from the big city.

Eventually we were able to find a physician right here in our hometown that did work with us as much as possible out side of the traditional medical model. Though she couldn't apply the alternative treatment protocol that we were using, she could order up blood tests for us. This really was a bonus for us, as it would save us hours of having to travel out of town to get these preliminary procedures accomplished.

This doctor, though not an expert in working with autistic children, understood the prevailing symptom of anxiety often displayed and she did a stellar job of making Hadley's office visits as favorable as possible.

One time she really helped us out. Hadley was

scheduled to have a blood draw at the local lab. This reputable doctor called ahead to the hospital staff before we had arrived and suggested that the technicians take off their (white jackets) uniforms and instead just wear their normal casual clothes. This astute gesture worked brilliantly, successfully setting a calm non-medical tone and relaxed our Hadley. I was grateful for the extra effort from the staff and their compliance to help us out. Though we had to get eight vials filled that day not one drop of blood was spilled. It was another large victory for a small town community.

Looking back and reminiscing on stories from the past, Hadley, being able to finally express herself, remembers that experience quite another way:

"Mom, how old was I when we got my first blood draw, was I in the first grade or the second grade?" she asked. (Hadley always gives you a choice for the answer when asking a question. She already knows the answer but insists on asking anyway. Usually we answer wrong and she then sharply corrects us.)

"I think first grade," I answered with my best guess.

"No, the second!" she reprimanded.

"Yes, you're right Hadley, it must have been the second grade." I apologized. I, not having the same photographic memory, could not remember the right answer.

"Don't you remember?" She continued. "I fainted!" Hadley declared. "I fainted right there on that bed.

"There were six nurses holding me down and I was kicking and screaming like a wild bronco!"

I gulped at her vivid recall and detailed dramatization.

"Then you were holding my legs down and crying and

yelling out my name, 'Hadley, Hadley! Come back!'" she went on.

"And then Dad had to sit right on my head!"

Oh my, I thought to myself, Did all of that really happen? Is this really how she remembers all of that? Have I just blocked out the years of torment? How many other fabricated stories of torture are locked up in her little memory? And who would she tell them to?

Years later…

"Mom, listen to that little kid screaming in that room," my eighteen-year old Hadley said while waiting for her appointment.

"I used to do that, I used to be afraid, but not any more," she prided herself as we waited for her doctor to come into the exam room.

"Hey Doctor," Hadley called out to the woman who entered the room, "do you want me to make a fist like this?" she asked, pumping her fist with expertly rolled up sleeve.

"That would be great Hadley," the P.A. laughed. "I really love your cooperative attitude and I especially love how you refer to all of us nurses as your doctor!"

Who'd of ever thought that we would be having so much fun and laughs at the doctors' office, I asked Hadley. And when you pass through the valley of weeping you will be refreshed and you will grow stronger. Psalm 84: 5-7.

Hadley is much stronger now as she continues to endure this laborious but necessary treatment with such maturity and expertise. She calls herself the human pincushion but realizes that the benefits of her healing are so worth it.

I spoke with hundreds of parents of children who were recovering on this biomedical plan. For us, this plan was working and we did not see it as being a sham or harmful to our kids. It all reminded me of a story in the Bible where a blind man came up to Jesus and asked to be healed. The Bible tells us that the blind man, after being healed, replied, "He mixed mud with his spittle and now I see." (John 9:13)

The Payment

"Miss, I don't care about your financial status. My first question to you is what kind of insurance do you have? Yeah, yeah, yeah, I have heard it all before, the sob stories of your insufficient health care plan," the secretary droned on. "But that's neither my concern nor the doctor's. Imagine if the doctor didn't get paid and had to just write it off, well, he'd go out of business in no time. Step aside. Next."

I nervously crept up to the merciless receptionist. I couldn't believe what I was hearing. The receptionist could care less about the poor saps sitting so politely in the waiting room. I guess it wasn't her job. Her only loyalty seemed to be with the doctor and how he would be compensated. I pulled out my health card with trepidation and wondered if I would have better luck than the unfortunate one before me. *Not to worry*, I calmly told myself. *I have a plan. I'm no dummy.* I had done my homework after all. Didn't the insurance company tell me that all I needed to do was get a referral from my primary physician, present it to my doctor of choice, and I would get half of the coverage? The insurance agent had been so proud of herself because I was so happy to be going to get at least half of the coverage for the visit, as if assuring herself by saying, "We really are good people. Those other consumers just have the wrong perception of us that's all."

As for me, all I wanted to do was use my insurance, period. Since we were self-employed, it cost us fifteen thousand dollars each year for our family plan. Surely, there must be some benefit for us in there at that hefty cost. And besides, if I'm not using the money then who is?

My eyes came back into focus as my unbelieving ears burned from the pompous, power-wielding receptionist's arrogant tone.

"Today's visit will be two hundred dollars," she snapped.

"What?" I cried. "I was just here last week and I only paid one hundred."

"Last week you paid out of pocket. The rate is different today because you are using your insurance with a PPO referral," she shrieked annoyingly like a broken record.

The week prior I had paid out of pocket, not realizing that I had the opportunity to get a physician's referral, and the tyrant gladly took my cash. I figured that this week's visit would be half the amount since I was able to get a referral from my primary physician. Oh no, there would be no outsmarting this clever bunch. Because of the referral process, to actually use my insurance card the rate per hour for the consultation went up $100. What on earth is going on here? Either way you slice it, I was going to be out a

$100. Where does the $15,000 that I pay each year go? This is an atrocity! Like thousands of others in the country using alternative treatment methods, I was left paying hugely out of pocket whether I had insurance or not. I guess it would have been easier to have just taken the covered, free drugs suggested by the physician within my insurance network. But I don't know for whom—Hadley or me.

It is easy to see why some simply just do without the treatment period. *What kind of scam am I caught up in?* I shook my head as my numb body walked out of the cold, unjust circumstances that I had found myself in.

I thought to myself, *So much for my PPO referral benefit.* The insurance agent failed to tell me that tidbit of information, you know, the bit about the fact that the rules change and usually not to your benefit. Apparently the physician can charge one fee for out of pocket and another fee if the insurance will cover. They finally got me. They pulled out all the stops. They showed me. How dare I try to utilize my insurance benefits? This was yet another part of the frustration of seeking medical treatment for an autistic child.

Just when it seemed that we were coming up for air, breathing again, on this unbelievable journey with our precious Hadley, it seemed that we could never stay above the surface. The Bible states that we should "give to Caesar what is Caesar's" (Matthew 22:21). For us the cost for treatment would not be an obstacle. We were going to do whatever it took to keep on this divine road to recovery.

Many states and insurance companies throughout the country are finally getting on board and demanding that insurance companies provide coverage for therapies and treatment for autism. We have such a long way to go but at least the ball is rolling. Psalm 27:14 says, "Wait for the Lord, be strong, and let your heart take courage; yes, wait for the Lord!"

Another Day at the Office

This time the story is not about the fleecing of my pocket book regarding treatment for Hadley, but the nightmare of the procedure itself. Going to the dentist can be a traumatic experience for people of all ages and dispositions. For the autistic person, multiply that experience by one hundred. We had just had a great trip to the dentist. Hadley was finally able, after twelve years, to sit for a simple check-up without having to go to the hospital and be put under anesthesia. Hadley sat there like a champion while the dentist told us there were no cavities; however, we should be concerned about the wisdom teeth coming to the surface and the slight possibility of an abscess.

"Just keep an eye on it," we were told by our dentist. "Everything should be fine, at least until I am back from holiday break, and we will deal with all of these issues when I return."

We were accustomed to a two to three-hour visit in the hospital regarding any dental procedures, much less procedures that would be considered complicated.

"If any problems arise in the next few days, just let me know," said the dentist.

$100. Where does the $15,000 that I pay each year go? This is an atrocity! Like thousands of others in the country using alternative treatment methods, I was left paying hugely out of pocket whether I had insurance or not. I guess it would have been easier to have just taken the covered, free drugs suggested by the physician within my insurance network. But I don't know for whom—Hadley or me.

It is easy to see why some simply just do without the treatment period. *What kind of scam am I caught up in?* I shook my head as my numb body walked out of the cold, unjust circumstances that I had found myself in.

I thought to myself, *So much for my PPO referral benefit.* The insurance agent failed to tell me that tidbit of information, you know, the bit about the fact that the rules change and usually not to your benefit. Apparently the physician can charge one fee for out of pocket and another fee if the insurance will cover. They finally got me. They pulled out all the stops. They showed me. How dare I try to utilize my insurance benefits? This was yet another part of the frustration of seeking medical treatment for an autistic child.

Just when it seemed that we were coming up for air, breathing again, on this unbelievable journey with our precious Hadley, it seemed that we could never stay above the surface. The Bible states that we should "give to Caesar what is Caesar's" (Matthew 22:21). For us the cost for treatment would not be an obstacle. We were going to do whatever it took to keep on this divine road to recovery.

Many states and insurance companies throughout the country are finally getting on board and demanding that insurance companies provide coverage for therapies and treatment for autism. We have such a long way to go but at least the ball is rolling. Psalm 27:14 says, "Wait for the Lord, be strong, and let your heart take courage; yes, wait for the Lord!"

Another Day at the Office

This time the story is not about the fleecing of my pocket book regarding treatment for Hadley, but the nightmare of the procedure itself. Going to the dentist can be a traumatic experience for people of all ages and dispositions. For the autistic person, multiply that experience by one hundred. We had just had a great trip to the dentist. Hadley was finally able, after twelve years, to sit for a simple check-up without having to go to the hospital and be put under anesthesia. Hadley sat there like a champion while the dentist told us there were no cavities; however, we should be concerned about the wisdom teeth coming to the surface and the slight possibility of an abscess.

"Just keep an eye on it," we were told by our dentist. "Everything should be fine, at least until I am back from holiday break, and we will deal with all of these issues when I return."

We were accustomed to a two to three-hour visit in the hospital regarding any dental procedures, much less procedures that would be considered complicated.

"If any problems arise in the next few days, just let me know," said the dentist.

I didn't give that notion another thought, as Hadley seemed to be just fine during our Christmas break. We went about on our usual vacation routine of staying up late and watching our favorite movies. We baked gluten-free cookies and decorated ginger bread houses. We went sledding until our toes were numb from the cold.

"More dairy-free hot chocolate, honey?" I asked.

"Yes." She happily nodded.

Oh, how I love the relaxing slow pace of the holidays, I thought.

"How about tomorrow we spend the day building that Victorian doll house?" I asked.

It was the afternoon of New Year's Eve and I was in party mode. I was anticipating my usual thirty-some guests. I dashed about the house to make sure that everything was presentable and in place. The party CDs were stacked and ready to play. The devilled eggs topped with caviar along with eggnog were all prepared and chilling in the fridge.

"Okay Hadley, I am finally ready to set up your dollhouse." Hadley came running down from her room making the horrible sound from a child that no mother wants to hear.

"Oucheeeeee! My toof! My toof!" Hadley cried out in pain.

"Oh, Lord," I said with dread.

Those famous last words of the doctor rang in my head: "If any problems arise, just let me know."

Oh dear, I concluded, *this year we won't be singing "Auld Lang Syne" with our friends but instead with the dentist and her staff. We are certainly heading for an unexpected brief visit to the hospital.*

Hadley continued to scream and cry as she was in obvious real pain.

I tried for two hours to get a hold of our dentist with no success. Our dentist that was familiar with working with autistic kids. Our dentist that was familiar with Hadley. Our dentist that was unshakable and calm no matter what bizarre performance was displayed.

"No, ma'am, the dentist is gone on holiday. However, we will set you up with the on-call dentist," the operator stated.

"But this is Hadley we are talking about. She is a very special child," I cried. "He won't know how to deal with her."

Oh dear, what could we do? I thought as my blood pressure began to climb. We had no other choice. Hadley's pain was increasingly getting worse by the hour. She had spiked a high fever. Something needed to be done and quickly. With screaming child in tow, clutching her beloved Lamb Chop doll, we battled the ice-slicked roads and made the long two-hour trek to the dentist office on the afternoon of New Year's Eve.

We tried to calm ourselves and just be thankful that we were getting Hadley taken care of. What could go wrong? But as we walked into the new office, we noticed that things were quite different. Where were the shelves of stuffed animals? Where was the giant fish tank? Where were the brightly colored murals on the walls? Besides the fact that this office looked very formal and professional, not at all kid friendly, we would be okay we assured our selves. Just because we were not handed any headphones that played music to help calm Hadley down, she would be fine. We were in professional hands. What could possibly go wrong? We were ushered into the very small room with very scary machinery all over the place. We were getting that all too familiar look from all the staff. You know the one that implies, "Isn't there any way you can quiet that kid? She is frightening all of the other patients out in the lobby."

Everything seemed to be happening so fast. I was frantically trying to give some sort of life history on this child in the few minutes that I had. Some sort of explanation had to be given to these strangers. This is a child that has to be put under with anesthesia to have the slightest procedure. Up to this point, she was barely even able to sit for a cleaning. Her autism had afforded her a very low threshold for pain, not to mention very high anxiety. This is a kid who ran around the house wearing her red-and-green plaid knee high rubber boots for a week one time because we wanted to simply clip her toenails. In her clever little mind, she figured the boots would ward us off.

"Now, now, don't you worry; we have to get at that abscess, which happens to be right under the wisdom tooth coming up to the surface," the gentle dentist informed us.

"Not a problem," he went on. "We will give a local anesthetic and address both issues at once, and you will be home in no time and on you're way to ringing in the New Year with all of your friends."

Oh dear, should we call the whole thing off ? Should we grab our terrified baby and run for our lives? This isn't how we usually do things. She has never been awake for an abstraction or drill ever in her life. She will not be prepared to handle this. No room for discussion. By the time those thoughts were leaving my head, the professionals were hooking our baby's arm up to the monitor. Bill and I had just about fainted from the anxiety of it all.

Dear Lord, please help us to get through this, I pleaded. This is so out of the ordinary for us. We usually go to the hospital for all of her procedures. Everything seemed to be happening so fast. It didn't seem to matter that we had some very special needs to address. The professionals began their work.

As things got underway, I couldn't tell who was screaming louder, Hadley or me. The heart monitor was beeping frantically louder and louder as if it had known every raw nerve in Hadley's body. *Dear Jesus, please help my baby get through this*, I begged.

Hadley was as white as a corpse. The dentist was doing his absolute best with this very uncooperative patient. I had never witnessed her face looking so lifeless, along with the fact that her death grip on the armchair exposed her knuckles to be lily white. She shook her sweet head back and forth like a wild animal determined not to let the enemy in. It took three of us to hold her still.

Dear God, please don't take her away from us.

"Beep! Beep! Beep!" sounded the monitor faster and faster. *Her anxiety is going to launch her into a heart attack*, I feared.

There we were watching our baby strapped into what looked like a torture chamber holding her down as she thrashed about. The shot of local anesthesia they had given her had made her entire arm swell up to the size of a football.

"Is there some reason as to why her arm is the size of a football?" I screamed at the dentist who appeared to be oblivious to this nightmarish sight.

"We missed the vein but she will be fine," he said confidently.

"So basically what you are saying," I screamed, "is that this precious baby is literally being, in her mind, tortured without the aid of any anesthesia?"

"She will be just fine," he replied unruffled and just kept on working.

"She is simply, helplessly enduring!" I yelled back at him.

Hadley's terrified, desperate eyes launched a spear right through my heart. That horrified expression on that sweet face is still etched upon my brain to this day. *My God, what have I done to my baby?*

Bill was trying his best to hold down Hadley's legs and feet. She was thrashing and kicking and almost leaping up out of her chair. Two or three others were gathered around her face, trying drastically to insert the largest, sharpest looking instruments into her tightly closed mouth. Though to us the conditions appeared grim, these professionals were confident and continued to work diligently.

Tears streaming down our faces, Bill and I began to sing sweet hymns to our baby all the while crying out, *Dear God, are you here? Please be here. Help my baby pull through this.* But she just kept on screaming and thrashing about.

"Almost done, sweetheart," the dentist said. "You are a real trooper."

"Beep, beep, beep," continued the annoying monitor.

"In this world, there will be trouble, but you said you would go through it with us," I fretfully muttered to myself.

Finally, after what seemed like hours of pure hell, Hadley began to feel less tense, and I eventually released my tight grip on her arm. The monitor slowed to a more normal-sounding rate. This surreal experience was coming to a close. *I think we're going to make it.* Bill and I buried our heads on our baby's chest, laying over her like worn-out dishrags. *Thank you, God. Thank you.*

"Finished!" the dentist announced with triumph. He wiped his brow and gave his staff an assuring look as if to say, "We've really earned our pay checks today!"

I glanced at the clock on the wall. Could it be possible that what had appeared to be a lifetime of torture and horror was really only about forty-five minutes? Probably just another day's work for the impetuous professionals, but for us, it was just one more traumatic day at the office.

Be still and know that I am God.

Psalms 46:10

The Facts

The fact *is* that Hadley was born perfectly normal. The doctor said so when he handed her to me. The very first months of her life, our baby looked us in the eyes. She smiled at us and made acknowledging cooing noises to indicate that she recognized us. She sang and responded to songs and games and played with toys. Our baby communicated with us and engaged the world around her. There did not appear to be any signs of anything being abnormal. So for us it was very hard to swallow the fact that she had suddenly, based on her gene makeup alone as some professionals were suggesting, become autistic at the age of three. Thinking back I remember the exact words of one professional: *"It is just your fate."*

The moment was rare when Bill and I could escape and be alone together. The kids were at the house with their big sister Lauren who was thirteen years older than them. She was well into her career and lived in another town. We all loved it when she would come for visits. The kids considered her to be their second mom because of the age difference. Grateful that the kids were all contented and engrossed in their movie, Bill and I hit the beach.

"Are you okay with the fact that I pulled you out of the city and made you move here?" I asked as we slowly walked along the sandy shore.

"It's so beautiful here," Bill said as he looked out over the vast stretch of aqua-blue water that was two short blocks from our house. "What it is now, seven years?" he asked.

"Eight actually, but who is counting?" I asked rhetorically. "No, I mean do you think that we did the right thing by moving here? Sometimes I can't help but wonder because we live so far away from what seems like civilization."

"Well, a mall would be nice. We are a long way from Bloomingdale's on Michigan Avenue, if that's what you mean," Bill teased.

Though we loved our new small town surroundings, we continued to ponder these questions for the first few years. There were so many adjustments to make living in a rural area. One of those adjustments was long distance travel, as we were very far now from people, places, and things.

I had to learn to use my resources wisely. The computer and the Internet became my closest friends. They would become my greatest tools for communication, research, and, of course, online shopping.

What a blessing, I thought, that I was no longer working outside of our home. I had all the time in the world it seemed to explore and continue my search for answers for my Hadley. And that is exactly what I did for hours each day after the kids left for school.

In the very beginning of this misadventure with Hadley, no one even uttered the word *autism* to us. And when they did, no one seemed to know what it meant or what to do about it. There was little to no information to be found anywhere on the matter. The professionals were as perplexed over this childhood phenomenon as the parents. The specialists evaluating our daughter appeared to be as puzzled over our dubious child as we were.

So eight years into our journey it was amazing to me that I could simply type in the word autism and over a dozen or more websites would appear. After years of unsuccessfully searching, there finally seemed to be innumerable sites providing definitions, theories, and treatment plans regarding autism. There were even sites offering information on *alternative* medical standards, and of course genetics and how they may or may not relate to autism. If you are willing to do the work the information is there. Having spent hours reading it all, I discovered that the arguments vary and the theories are vast. I am still not quite convinced as to any one culprit being sole responsible but rather a combination of variables to bring about the demise of autism.

In weighing the facts, one is free to choose what to

believe. I believe something terrible happened along the way to our beautiful, healthy baby. It may have had something to do with genes as far as her DNA is concerned, but I believe it also had very much to do with the heavy metals and toxins administered to her through her vaccinations. She may not have had the right DNA makeup to withstand or rid the toxins found in vaccinations from her body as they were intended.

Bill and I are just not that wide-eyed to believe that, suddenly, at a given point in time, our baby, between the ages of two to three, having been told being perfectly normal at birth, stopped being normal and suddenly became, by genetics alone, autistic. In all my research, I found no such autism gene, so what on earth happened? Somewhere in her very young age, I believe that a culprit was introduced.

Through our research we discovered that mercury had been used as a preservative in childhood vaccinations for the past three decades. We know that vaccinations can be produced and used without adding mercury, but apparently it is not cost effective. It is used as a preservative to instill a long shelf life. How ironic, since I believe it can stunt the shelf life of a child. I am not against vaccinations being used; I am just against the amount of and the consistent schedule in which they are administered. I don't understand why a baby would need to have 3-4 shots per month from birth to age three. What kind of a world do we live in that would demand that kind of protection? I think that vaccinations have a place but we have gone over board.

Vaccinations have been known to comprise such

noxious substances as mercury, aluminum and formaldehyde. Anyone can ask to read the product description of a vaccination; you'll be surprised at what you find in it. Also you might want to give yourself a good half hour to read the rather lengthy document. And, it wouldn't hurt to have a magnifying glass handy; as it is the tiniest print you will ever read.

We had our Hadley tested and found that she had high amounts of mercury and lead in her blood system. How did so much mercury invade our child's system, and why wasn't her body able to eliminate it? Environmentalists rant continuously about the effects of mercury and toxins imposing our world. If these toxins can be dangerous to the environment, I thought, then why on earth would we put them directly into our human bodies?

The more I researched, the more I began to wonder about mercury and what the possible affects it could have had on Hadley's immune system. I pondered the feasibility of the noxiousness of mercury and how it might harm her physically and mentally. Our normal baby was suddenly, out of nowhere, displaying developmental and behavioral regression. Even worse was that she seemed to be in constant physical pain and no one was able to relieve it for her.

We agonized over the onset of her regressive autism as it just happened to be lined up with the time that Hadley had finished her vaccination schedule. Hadn't I noticed that she seemed to be slipping away month after month?

What little I knew about mercury from research led me to believe that even small amounts in the blood system could cause significant disorders in the brain as well as in the immune system. The high amounts we discovered in our daughter's system convinced us. It certainly might explain her bizarre conduct of impaired cognitive development, hand-flapping, toe-walking, loss of eye contact, loss of speech, as well as her physical symptoms that caused her extreme gastrointestinal discomfort.

Bill and I do not believe that a predisposed gene caused these problems alone because she was absolutely normal at one time. We believe the heavy toxins, found in her test results, played a significant role in interrupting her normal development. The evidence seemed clear to us because, once we began the process of (chelation), elimination of the heavy metals that were found in her body, we began to see dramatic changes. We began adding in the nutrients and vitamins that had been depleted from her system by the heavy metals, and we were on our way to recovery. It was like the brakes on a bicycle had been unlocked on Hadley's neurodevelopment, our doctor explained. She was able to focus again. She was finally able to receive information and send it back out. She was beginning to process information. Hadley stopped flapping her arms and began walking on her feet rather than her toes. She was finally starting to connect with her environment. Hadley began to come back to us.

As I said above, before the age of three, our Hadley was a very vibrant, happy, engaging baby. She made sweet eye contact with us. She hugged and played with us. When I held her, she would look dreamily into my eyes. She laughed and cried appropriately in situations. In fact, the pediatrician had informed us that she was meeting all of her normal developmental milestones. *So what happened? What is autism anyway?* we continued to ask ourselves. *Where does the term come from?* Dr. Bernard Rimland, Ph.D, once referred to it as "daydreaming."[4]

It wasn't until the next few years that she would begin to appear to be constantly "daydreaming." Something had clearly changed. She was no longer with us, simply there but not there.

Bill and I continued to wonder about this mysterious *autism*. Where did our baby girl go? What on earth happened to her? And why can't anybody seem to help us or give us any information? We feared that no one would answer those questions, and then the help for Hadley could be hindered. That hindrance for recovery was five years. Does someone know the truth of what's happening to our babies? I once heard it said at a parent meeting that truths about disabilities are sometimes bitterly fought and even denied before the actual truth is known. We wanted to know the truth.

Though still a mystery, there really is so much more information now on autism. If you put the time into it you will most likely find results that best meet your needs. One of the greatest discoveries for me while travelling that Internet highway was coming across the advocacy and parent groups that I found. I actually began having conversations with other parents who also had autistic children. Now, as I stated before, there are volumes of didactic information to consider, but there is no comparison to evaluating and discussing real, tried and true information from other people. Besides, the "theories," though they all had similarities, I could find no conclusive agreements. Preferably, I found myself talking to other moms and dads from all over the country. I was learning how they were coping and what methods they were applying to their children. There is nothing better than getting information from the experts, the parents. It was through those parents that I had learned about the conferences.

"Don't worry, Mary Ann, the kids will be fine with your mom. Besides, we will only be gone for two and a half days," Bill assured me.

"I know," I replied. "And maybe we will even run into our doctor again like we did at the last conference.

"Wasn't it great to know that he was there learning at the same rate as us of the latest interventions for our Hadley?" I asked.

I compartmentalized my separation anxiety and let my mind drift to a lighter note. Bill patiently drove on our four-hour trek to attend the informational conference on Bio-Medical Treatment Options for autism. This would be our third trip within two years to a major city to attend the conference. During those long drives I would reflect on how blessed that I was to have a husband who would be so willing to explore everything and anything to further the quality of life for our precious daughter. Unfortunately, not every marriage is able to endure the trials of raising a child with disabilities, as the divorce rate is extremely high for couples with kids on the spectrum. Years earlier, Bill was much too busy to put much time into the research and travel. He relied on me and gave me his full support. But now that he was actively involved, it seemed that we had so much more power and steam behind the road to recovery for Hadley.

Yes, we were on our way to yet another conference together. The parents that I had met over the Internet highly encouraged us to attend. These conferences turned out to be a haven—a safe place where we all felt like we were on the same planet speaking the same language. Bill and I couldn't take notes fast enough as we learned of the cutting edge theories on bio-medical interventions. There were workshops on speech therapy, research initiatives, and parent panel discussions. We learned of possible genetic influences and their relationship to how one responds to the environment. The conferences allowed camaraderie amongst us parents of genuine love and understanding. There was a sense of hope and a desire to never give up. Though we all came from different corners of the earth, most of us had one thing in common. That one thing was that our children were normal at birth.

Even within the parent community, there is disagreement as to whether or not their child was born with or developed into regressive autism. The bad news is that children have been directly affected. The good news is that people of all camps are making noise about it. Think tanks of a variety of professionals and disciplines are putting their ideas and talents together to try to slay this dragon.

Along with our Hadley, many children are accurately being treated for their "autistic-like symptoms." I know this because I have spoken with so many parents at autism conferences across the country. These parents used the same treatment methods as we did, and they report that their children too are on the mend. For Hadley the biomedical treatment solutions proved best. Hadley, though recovering, is not completely cured by any means, but the hope for recovery lies somewhere in these facts.

Intentions may start out for the good of man, but, unfortunately, anything that man puts his hand upon has room for error. Once again we found ourselves trusting in a power higher than ourselves. We took hold of God's hand as we tried to navigate our way through our circumstances, trials, and despair. We found that nothing was too difficult for God to handle; we just had to believe. God began leading us to people and places that were able to help us. Miracles headed our way and that's a fact.

In this world, there will be trouble and sorrows. But take heart, because I have overcome the world.

John 16:33

The Healing

I love all the stories about healing in the Bible. They give me great hope. "'Do you want to be healed?' Jesus asked. 'Rise and take up your mat,' he replied" (John 5:6–9). Jesus spat on the ground and made clay and anointed the eyes of the blind man (John 9:13). I especially like that one because it sounds so organic and biomedical. Imagine what the insurance companies and the American Medical Association would have to say about that procedure.

There are so many stories emphasizing the compassion and the willingness of Jesus to heal people. As this chapter unfolds, you will discover how he divinely healed both Hadley and me. As believers we do not always tap into the authority that we have in Jesus' name. We try to muddle through things all by ourselves. Sometimes we don't even ask him for help. So many nights, I had cried out to God to help us, to heal our daughter. "Please, God, fix my baby," I would cry. God truly tells us to ask and we shall receive;

knock and the door will be opened (Matthew 7:7–9). I was pounding.

Do we really believe that our problems are too big for God? I sure did.

"It is your faith that has healed you," Jesus told the woman with the issue of blood (Matthew 9:20). This woman believed that if she could just reach out and touch the hem of the robe of Jesus, she would be healed. Like her, I was so desperate to grab a hold of something. I needed real power. Though each person in these bible stories had a different set of circumstances, the one thing they all had in common was their incredible amount of faith. Where had mine gone? Somewhere in my heart I knew it was there I just hadn't tapped into it in years. I begged God to take away the autism and because he didn't I was angry and I let go of my faith. Dismally I began to question whether I loved God for who he *is* or for what he could do for me?

It was time to set my priorities right and that included putting God first in my life, not my career, my house or what kind of kids I had. It was time to put my shelved faith back into action. We had been so focused on the healing of Hadley that we hadn't noticed the need for healing for ourselves. We were so distracted doing life that we carelessly tossed God aside in our day-to-day activity.

We loved God and we went to church. Yet by our human nature, we wanted to do things our own way, not his. It took the trials that were readily devouring us to realize just how much we needed him. I was ready and willing to finally ask for his help. Never again to retreat to our old selves with the attitude of "Okay, thanks, God, that was great, we can take it from here." Because the truth of the matter was that I knew that I couldn't *take it* anymore at all. In fact, trying to do this all by myself eventually landed me in the hospital with a brain tumor that almost killed me.

We needed God, and we were holding onto Him with both hands! I couldn't spend another minute pondering the "why" questions to my trials because that was just exhausting my time and energy. Why did this happen to us? Why did this happen to my baby? Why is my body falling apart? Why has all of this happened to us? Those questions kept me at the bottom of the sea, and I needed to return to the surface if I was going to be of any help to Hadley. As I drew closer to God, seeking him diligently I realized that the Almighty had his own purposes and they may not line up with mine.

The pondering of the "why" questions that I used to ask regarding my daughter's autism changed to "Why, God, had I dismissed you from my life? Why, God, hadn't I trusted you all of these years? Why did I drift away from you?"

We can make our plans but the Lord determines our steps. I had a great career and a wonderful husband. I was living in one of the most exciting cities in the world. We travelled to any place that we wanted to go. It seemed as though I could have had anything that my little heart desired. Because my world seemed so perfect, I guess I felt that I didn't need God. I knew that he was there but I just didn't make room for him.

I began spending time reading my Bible and talking to God again. I wanted to re-establish my relationship with the

God of the universe in a real personal way. Deep down in my soul I knew he was there. I tried everyone else for help, why not him. *My gosh*, I thought, *I need healing as much as Hadley does.*

God says that in this life there will be trouble (John 16:33). I can honestly admit that I don't know how I even coped without God, obviously I hadn't. I believe that sometimes God allows things to happen in order to get our attention. I had been a social worker for over fifteen years and had spent my life devoted to helping other people, but when it came to my own problems, instead of reaching out for much-needed help from others, I decided I could handle it all on my own. This proved to be a big mistake for me as I was in way over my head with this autism thing.

As a result, I internalized all of my anxiety and despair. As I explained in a previous chapter my health was beginning to fail, I was beginning to gain weight. I had been a distance runner but could no longer perform as my muscle tone continued to wane. I was depressed so I stopped taking care of myself. I gave little care to my once, well-put-together appearance. I was much too proud and arrogant to ask for the desperate help that I needed. I even tried to downplay it and pretend that all was well with friends and neighbors. But I was not adapting well at all to my steady stream of stress. Bill and I fought all the time as we struggled through the emotional turmoil of having a child with autism. I was trying to cope with a little girl who literally spent her days running, flapping, and screaming aimlessly through the house for no apparent reason. She was in constant pain as she kicked at the walls and pulled at her hair regularly. My precious little girl could not talk to me or tell me what was troubling her.

During those years, I had extremely poor concentration and couldn't seem to focus on any one thing. I often found myself donning crutches as my body continued to deteriorate. I was physically and mentally falling apart. Needless to say, my marriage was hanging on by a thread. I was in and out of doctors' offices demanding answers for me, as well as for my daughter, but getting nowhere fast. No one seemed to take a look at my overall problems but instead just kept treating my symptoms. How could I possibly take care of Hadley when I was literally coming apart at the seams?

It wasn't until after that move to the small town that I finally received a diagnosis of Cushing's disease. God continued to put the right people in my path to help us.

Whew! I wasn't actually losing my mind after all! I cried with elation. *I actually have something wrong with me, something very real to be causing all of this horror to my body and mind. Yeah! I have a brain tumor!* I rejoiced.

As nutty as it seemed, I couldn't have been happier with my diagnosis. You have to realize that I had frequented doctors' offices with little or no results for over three years and had developed the reputation of being quite the hypochondriac. In that small town, a doctor, who happened to be a friend of my husband's brother, had discovered the culprit to all my problems. I was diagnosed with Cushing's disease. Tests showed a tumor on my pituitary gland. Living with autism had caused my stress level to be highly taxed and overloaded, which kicked my adrenal glands into high gear. I was now in "fight or flight" mode, one of the functions we experience depending on how we are responding to our stress, my doctor explained.

"Maybe that explains 'The Move,'" I mused.

My physician continued to explain that the tumor was caused by the release of too much of a hormone called adrenocorticotropic. This hormone then began producing too much cortisol.

"It all sounds so technical," he said, "but it is basically induced by too much stress."

Then he looked me dead in the eye and asked, "Been under a little stress have we?"

Fortunately, I was able to have a successful operation, and though recovery was long and arduous, within a year's time my body and mind came back. And for the first time in a long time I felt as though I was amongst the living.

I believe that God created us and that he promises to take care of us. Thank God he was always patiently waiting for me to come back to him. One of the Bible's greatest truths is this: God never abandons us when life becomes too difficult. In fact, it took me almost a lifetime to realize that he was there all along. If only I had turned to him and renewed my strength from the start. He is always with us and wants to help us even when things have spun completely out of control.

He does not guarantee to reverse every misfortune or discomfort in our lives. He may not even change your circumstances but He *will* change you. Oh, how I wanted him to take away this autism and give me back my perfect baby. But that was not the plan, and we finally surrendered our lives to Christ and accepted our assignment. *"Nothing in all creation can separate us from the love of God that is in Christ Jesus our Lord"* (Romans 8:39).

Trust me, even though one has very carefully laid out plans for life as we did, God's way will prevail. God puts us in situations so that *his* will and divine purpose will be carried out, we just have to be willing to cooperate.

Yet no matter what my circumstances were, I decided that I wanted to lead a God-honoring life. I wanted my thoughts and actions to be pleasing to God. It took me several stubborn years to yield to that. I finally realized that Hadley was God's child, and that she mattered to him as well as to me. He loves her just the way she is, why can't I?

I began to realize that God wants *us* to be up close and personal with him and sometimes that involves lying something down. For me it was having a daughter *without* autism. I had to be willing to lay down my expectations for my daughter and pick up the plan that God designed for me through the autism. What an avenue of opportunity I realized that I had to advocate for others. I never would have guessed all those years ago that God would be able to use my mess for His platform to help point people to Him. I now have ammunition to give a message of hope and encouragement, strength, compassion, and love to those who are hurting, whether it is autism or not.

There just seems to be something about that child, Agent H, that really touches people. People were beginning to tell us things about her that would make our hearts soar.

"Oh, Mrs. Payne, I was a substitute in Hadley's class today at church. You should have heard your daughter. She prayed so tenderly and sweetly for all of us. In her prayer she mentioned people who most of us haven't thought about in years. She really touched our hearts this morning."

But living with and loving Hadley had given me the opportunity to also know God in ways and on a level that I never dreamed that I could. The trials that we had endured allowed me to grow in perseverance, strength, and character as I drew closer and trusted Him. I was really beginning to smile again.

"Okay, Hadley, we can sing your song again," I said as I grabbed my guitar.

It has been so long since I picked up that wonderful instrument, I thought to myself. I used to play and sing songs so long ago for the kids when they were little. In fact, sometimes when Hadley was really out of sorts I would just start playing as a last attempt to calm everyone down. Her response to the music would amaze me, as she would be almost mesmerized by it.

In a world of make believe, where nothing is real...
Is it hard to imagine, the way people feel...
People are infallible, and life goes on and on...
Life is like a circus wheel, it goes round and round
Ooh, la, la, la, Ooh, la, la, la

Hadley sang out loud as this was her favorite part of the song that I had written.

"That's awesome, Hadley. I can't believe that you remember the song," I said as we continued to sing together.

> *Well, you can see for miles when things are magic*
> *And you can see through eyes and things aren't tragic*
> *Ooh, ooh what a feeling, Momma*
> *My senses are reeling, Momma*
> *Birds are singing and there's no more tearing*
> *And everywhere is love*
> *I'm elated, what a feeling, in make believe above*
> *Why can't it?*
> *Can it be real?*
> *Ooh, ooh, la, la, la, Ooh, ooh, la, la, la*
> *Ooh, ooh, la, la, la, Ooh, ooh, la, la, la*

Hadley sang all the louder as she danced and giggled around the living room with her Lamb Chop doll. My baby girl and I were beginning to have fun.

"We passed you and Hadley the other day while driving to town, and you were both skipping and smiling down the street as if you didn't have a care in the world," our friends would remark, amazed that people could be so happy in spite of themselves. That peace that surpasses all understanding that the Bible talks about, well, I was beginning to feel it.

I began to believe that this beautiful little girl named Hadley was my ordained "assignment" from a holy God. It wasn't so much a trust for healing anymore but rather a trust for acceptance. My new motto became "This is who we are and this is what we do." I was finally beginning to accept my daughter and our "other" side of life.

I believe that God is able to heal and he is willing. If he wanted Hadley to be anything other than who she was, I truly believe that he would have done something about it, and who knows, maybe he still will. If he tells a mountain to move, it moves. God is the creator of all and nothing surprises him. The blind man by the pool, when he came face-to-face with Jesus, though he couldn't see him, believed that he would be healed (John 5:7).

Though Jesus wasn't standing physically right in front of me as with the blind man, I began to see Him in all of my surroundings. I saw him in the people that we came in contact with, the people he lined up to help us:

"Yes, Hadley can join our Girl Scout troop."

"Yes, Hadley can sing in the choir. She is just a joy and she enriches us all."

"Yes, Hadley can go on the camping trip. The other kids learn so much from being with her."

"Yes, we would love to have Hadley at our house on Tuesdays. We just love her and the things she says are just so funny. Why, we asked her just the other night what Mom and Dad were up to while she was over here with us and she replied, 'They are home watching adult movies.'"

We laughed so hard because we know that for Hadley that means that any movie that's not animated is considered an "adult" movie. Imagine what a stranger might think!

Those things that he allows to happen, he works together for the good of those who love God, who are called according to his purpose (Romans 8:28). Through the lives of others, we were starting to see God's divine purpose for Hadley. We, at home, affectionately call her Agent H. She just seemed to be the shot in the arm that everyone needed. (How ironic, since I believed that the shot in her arm from her vaccinations played a role in her regressive autism.)

Partnering up with God gave us hope and strength. He would begin to heal Hadley and me and fight our battles in ways far beyond our comprehension. All things are possible in his name. If he was with me, then who could be against me? That would be my quote every time I left the house with Hadley. I now had a mighty shield. The Bible is filled with examples of Jesus' healing power. I believe that the Lord has healed people in the past and is capable of healing them today and tomorrow.

God has healed Hadley in so many amazing ways. She talks to us now, reads books, rides a bike, laughs and tells jokes and has jobs in the community.

Hadley is the apple of God's eye. He holds her dear. He views her with value and purpose. Hadley loves people of all shapes and sizes. It doesn't matter to Hadley who you are or what kind of person you are. She will find good in you. She does not judge you because she will like you just for who you are. Hadley only sees the good in people. I wish I could be more like that. She will stop at the drop of a hat to pray for people. She prays with such intensity and sincerity that you can almost feel Jesus standing right there beside her. And if you use the word god outside of a prayer, she will be sure to tell you, "Hey, we don't say that. We say *gosh*."

Sometimes, out of exasperation, I have had to remind myself to stop and not scold. Let her repeat for the fifth time that Kim Possible, her favorite cartoon, will be on at 5:00 p.m. From many a nap I have been abruptly awakened only to realize that, no the house is not on fire, but that the urgency in Hadley's voice is just reminding me that Kim Possible is now starting on TV.

"Mom, Mom, you must get up. It is time for Kim Possible!"

"Yes, baby, I'm up, I'm up. Yes, let's watch your show."

"Yes, Mom, let's watch my show," she would repeat as she squealed with delight while clutching her Lamb Chop doll. Lamb Chop is Hadley's BFF and I must tell how they met.

We all identify with someone in our lives. Eminent individuals have been known to influence people, whether an athlete, politician, writer, theologian, actor, singer, you name it; it could even be plain old Grandpa.

Significant people have helped shape, mold and encourage others to strive to be who they themselves may aspire to be.

Wouldn't you know that for Hadley that significant person was a white furry talking lamb?

When Hadley was four years old she couldn't talk or even tie her shoes but she could expertly navigate the television remote and surf the thirty channels of our very complicated entertainment center.

"Oh rats, I cried, how do I switch from video back to regular TV mode?"

I was never good with the electronics in our home and if Bill happened to be out of town, should there be a glitch, I was doomed.

Amazingly, Hadley would notice my dilemma, waddle over to me without speaking, and take the remote from my useless hands. She would aim the remote, click, click, click and bam we were back in business.

A phenomenon I will never understand this side of heaven. The child couldn't even speak, never had a coarse in technology, did I mention, couldn't tie her shoes? But could operate this very high tech complicated entertainment center. Truthfully, I miss the simpler technology of "off and on." Why so complicated now? Why three remotes to turn on one television set? Why can't I figure out the mechanisms to make it work and how come she can?

Who taught her?

No one taught her, she just instinctively seemed to understand the technological details. There are some perks in being autistic.

And I thanked God because that TV, her technological friend, alleviated the emptiness of her lonely childhood. She would surf the channels for friends and it was as if the TV had sprouted arms scooping her up, pulling her right into its magical fantasy world. Since she had no friends to play with or programs to belong to the TV became her social outlet. We were safe in our home. We could be who we were, oddities and all. Hadley could be entertained, sustained, and satisfied for hours on end.

I felt guilty of being labeled a bad mom by allowing my daughter so much time in front of the tube. But something positive was beginning to happen. Hadley was relating to the sights, sounds and words of the characters from the shows that she was watching. She was beginning to evolve, as if she were stepping out of her autism.

There was one particular program that was really tapping into to Hadley's unemotional, robotic little self. The star of the show was commanding Hadley's full attention. I wasn't about to pull the plug or stop her from the one and only thing that was grabbing her attention. This was a miracle! This was the first time in her life, at age four, that she expressed enthusiasm in any thing. Hadley was *finally* taking an interest in something that seemed normal. Coming from a little girl who wouldn't even hold a dolly this was a miracle.

"Here Hadley, look what Mama brought for you, a sweet little dolly" I desperately lured years ago.

"Hey Hadley, lets build a house with my new Legos," Jack would coax.

But Hadley remained stony-eyed. She was completely oblivious to the wide assortment of merchandise that would have sent most kids' souls reeling.

So when Hadley discovered the TV show, *Lamb Chop Play Along* hosted by Shari Lewis, I couldn't have been happier. Each afternoon Hadley and I would curl up together and promptly tune in to channel 8. We finally had a mommy daughter activity, we were bonding and I have to say those were some of the happiest moments in my life. We danced around the living room floor together singing along with Shari as she masterfully taught her viewers incredibly wonderful complex words.

"DE LECT A BLE... IN QUIS I TIVE..." she would sing out for us to mimic in melodic tune as we successfully sang back. Hadley's gleeful face proved her joy as if even she was elated to here the sound of her own voice.

"This is the big word... song..."

Shari twirled and danced about as she continued to belt out the nouns teaching her audience.

I couldn't believe the transformation manifesting itself in Hadley as she flashed the sparkle in her large brown eyes that had been absent since birth. She was actually singing and forming words from her mouth as well as displaying an ear-to-ear smile across her cherub face. Shari was marvelous as she was so animated, colorful and funny. How she was able to prompt my autistic daughter to participate in her television classroom was nothing short of a miracle. She had so much energy and enthusiasm it was hard for even me to sit still.

The ingenious inclusion of Shari's puppet band of furry friends was absolutely brilliant. They taught Hadley how to converse, spell words, and accumulate a vast vocabulary. At the same time she was learning and singing songs, bantering conversation and telling jokes. It was likened to school but on the playground (recess) rather than in a stiff classroom setting. The fix that Shari's Lamb Chop had on my daughter was hypnotic as we continued to tune in week after week. This was my Hadley, the child who couldn't tell me how she felt or what she wanted for breakfast but suddenly could spell such words as despicable and direction. Shari introduced Lamb Chop, Charlie Horse and Hush Puppy to Hadley and they became her best friends.

Over the years we purchased all of the furry puppets and they have taken up residency in Hadley's life. A lot of kids on the autism spectrum are highly motivated by visual aids and these puppets impacted Hadley's life.

For the first time Hadley was twirling and spinning with a purpose, not in the aimless, absent-minded old way.

She was interacting with Lamb chop as though she was her BFF and I realized at that moment that Hadley was teachable and trainable.

"I love the ca sound ca… ca… ca…," Hadley sang as she danced around the room with Lamb chop.

"I love the ca sound, cuz that spells cat…"

Thank you, Shari, for using your talents and Lamb Chop to impact my Hadley at a time when no one else could. I attribute her love for reading, singing, and even her uncanny sense of humor to you.

I have to remind myself that it wasn't all that long ago that I cried out on my sofa each morning, "Oh please, Lord, let her just say something, anything. Let me hear the sound of her voice. Let me hear her say, 'Good morning, Mommy.' Oh please, Lord, please. How long must I wait?"

It would be another five years from that time before God answered my cries. But Hadley talked nonstop now, and though I knew it drove other people crazy, it was music to my ears.

"Come on, Jack boy, let's sword fight," Hadley begged her brother.

"Okay, Hadley, on guard," he commanded as he tossed her the Styrofoam weapons.

"Oh, I got you right in the guts." She laughed as she

lunged toward him.

"Oh yeah, well take that." Jack laughed back as he clunked her on the head with the flexible sword. And off they chased each other through the house as though they were re-enacting scenes from *Pirates of the Caribbean*.

It is answered prayer. It is a modern-day miracle because weren't we told repeatedly by doctors that Hadley would never speak? That this was just our fate in life and that we had better just accept it? Yet these things happen so that others can see the mighty power of the Lord!

Our portion is according to our individual faith. Faith is the substance of things hoped for. Believing that you have that which you cannot see. It's amazing how large your faith becomes when you find yourself in a position of desperation. I desperately wanted healing for my beautiful little girl. The word *perfect* echoed in my ears. It was the word the doctor had used to describe Hadley as he delivered her.

But some time between her birth and the age of three something had gone terribly wrong. I was determined to spend the rest of my life, if that's how long it would take, to figure this out. Even when it literally almost killed me! I knew that I could not slay this dragon on my own; it would require the help of a higher being. That is when I surrendered my life fully to God. That was the turning point and the beginning of the healing for the rest of us. Hadley may not be completely healed by the world's standards, but then again, wasn't it the world that once told me that she would never be able to talk? And talk she does ever so eloquently.

Hadley is obsessed with Disney movies and of course all the princesses. For years when she was locked up in her own (tower) world and couldn't talk, these animated characters were her best friends in which she strongly identified. So strongly that on one night she transformed herself into Mulan.

"Hey, Bill, don't forget about tonight. I have to be at the parent meeting for a few hours and I need you to watch Hadley," I said.

What a lucky break. Bill was actually in town this week and I didn't have to get a babysitter. I grabbed my keys and happily skipped out the door. Three hours later as I returned to my happy home, I was thinking, *Oh, I bet that had and dad are playing Uno or maybe even baking gluten-free chocolate chip cookies. How wonderful to have Daddy home for a change during the week.*

"Hey guys, I'm home," I called as I opened the door. In came running toward me, like a bolt of lightning, a child with very, very short hair grinning from ear to ear.

"Hi, Mommy, I am your son," cried the elated person.

"Bill!" I screamed as I stared at the face of the person that I couldn't recognize. I dropped my purse to the ground and tried to steady myself. I knew that Hadley's latest obsession was with the movie *Mulan*, but I never dreamt that she would go to these measures. Later I would discover that Mulan had cut off all her hair in order to join the army to fight for freedom.

It was ingenious how Hadley was able to pull it off with such precision—a perfect boy's crew cut all on her own without ever having attended beauty school. Only Hadley would have the ingenuity to strategically go into my bathroom to angle the mirror in order to skillfully cut the left side of her hair and then go into her own bathroom to angle the mirror to cut the right side. The piles of neatly stacked-up hair still remained on the sink as evidence.

As for Bill, he sheepishly put the scissors away and apologized for falling asleep. It was amazing how nice the new 'do actually looked after we got over the shock of it.

Hadley can repeat the dialog from movies verbatim and will often break into song right on cue and on perfect pitch when the song in the movie presents itself.

She has a unique and dramatic way of incorporating the dialogue from these movies and inserting them into our everyday normal conversations with people. Sometimes it is spot-on and sometimes it gets us into trouble, such as on the night we decided to take Hadley and the boys out to dinner and a show.

"I loved the part when the black knight gets his arm cut off," Jack said as he and Alan, our "adopted" son, laughed over their favorite scene from *Monty Python's Holy Grail*.

Hadley simply adored her two big brothers. Alan and Jack were best friends since the fifth grade. During the summer before Alan's senior year, his mom had to take a job in another town. Alan desperately wanted to finish out with his classmates. One conversation led to another and he moved in with us. From that moment on, Alan affectionately became known as our adopted son. After all those years of silence in our home, Bill and I agreed, what's one more—the more noise the merrier.

"It's merely a flesh wound," Bill roared in his best

British accent as he got in on the fun exchange from the play that we had just come from that night.

"Oh, that's my favorite part," chimed in the waitress as she approached our table.

The young waitress was laughing as she informed us that she had seen the play the night before. She stretched across the table with her tray to serve our drinks when suddenly down went the tray with Cokes splashing on us.

"Why, you clumsy little fool!" came from Hadley's mouth without missing a beat.

The frenzied waitress just froze.

"Hadley, we don't say things like that," chided Jack.

"Oh, I am so sorry," the embarrassed waitress said as she began brushing us off with her towel.

"I am so sorry for what my daughter said, ma'am," I apologized as I helped her mop up the sticky mess with our napkins.

"Our little cherub is autistic, and well, that remark is straight out from one of her favorite movies, *Cinderella*, I believe."

"Oh yes, the stepmother." The good-natured girl finally laughed as she said her apologies to all of us.

"Yeah, Hadley, you really need to keep your movies to yourself," said Alan.

"Just the other night you gave us quite a fright when Jack, Nathan, and I were coming in late, quietly sneaking up the back steps. We thought that you were sound asleep. Then we heard this eerie voice call out. 'I walk on the edge. I laugh in the face of danger.' Then we heard a sinister laugh, 'Ha, ha, ha, ha!' (*The Lion King*). Poor Nathan jumped out of his skin and accidently stomped on your dumb doll that you left on the stairs. Your doll suddenly spoke out at us, 'Pick me up, Mommy,' and really scared the crap out of us." Alan chuckled as he retold the story. "Us guys were still laughing and stumbling on the dark stairs and probably making too much noise for you 'cause then you yelled out, 'I'm not going to kill you! I'm not going to kill you!' Then you yelled at the top of your lungs, 'Go to your room!' (*Lilo and Stitch*). That totally made us all laugh all the harder.

"'Okay, we are safe now,' I said to Nathan, trying my best to quickly explain about Hadley and her use of movie content.

"'What do you mean safe?' asked a trembling Nathan. 'I don't know if I want to stay over.'

"'We can sleep with ease now,' Alan assured him. 'We don't have to sleep with one eye open for our get away. You heard her. She said that she is not going to kill us!'"

Still sipping our Cokes and waiting for our dinner, Hadley asked, "What else, what else happened?" She giggled with elation and begged Alan to tell the story again.

"That was so awesome, Hadley. You really crack us up," Jack said to his sister as he remembered the hilarious event.

"But the best one was the time we were at Big Boy," he reminded us all at the table. "Don't you guys remember when that motorcycle gang came in and sat down right behind us in the booth?"

Jack went on to explain how Hadley slowly turned around facing the big, burly guys in the booth behind us.

"Looking them straight in the eyes, she said, 'You're lucky. Your mom lets you draw on your arms (*Arthur*).' Oh man, I didn't think we'd make it out of there alive." He laughed.

Hadley also has an uncanny ability to rename her friends as the characters she has come to know through these movies. The characters that she assigns people appear to fit the actual person's appearance as well as personality. Depending on who you are or what you look like, you could be renamed Shrek, Clara Belle Cow, Mrs. Pots, or Jasmine.

We all laugh hysterically because most of the time she is amazingly accurate!

She loves to have conversations with people on the telephone. Often she will pick up our church directory and just call people at random in order to have a conversation with them. It is amazing how often people will come up to me the next day and say, "I had a real nice conversation with Hadley last night."

"Oh?" I curiously respond.

Or better yet, someone would tell me that they had called to talk to me but Hadley answered the phone instead.

"Hi, Hadley," they would say.

"Hi," she would say back.

"Have you seen your mom?" In which Hadley would scan the living room and spot me reading on the sofa and reply, "Why yes," and then promptly hang up! Oh Agent H, how you make us laugh!

God is so good. He knows the whole picture when we only see the little parts in between. In the very beginning, with Hadley and her autism, we could not believe that this child would end up bringing us pure joy. God equips us with all that we need to survive in our own personal situations. If he puts you in a situation, he will give you all that you need to handle it. It may not be what you want or what you expected. It may not be at all what you had planned on. It most likely will not be easy, but it is an opportunity to just say, "Yes, Lord," and then get ready for the ride of a lifetime.

Imagine if Mary had said, "No way, God. I am not going to have anything to do with this plan of yours to birth your son." Instead she said yes, and God's plan was carried out. You can just imagine her thinking, "Okay, God, I said yes, now why on earth am I giving birth in a barn?"

Lean not on our understanding but fully depend on the ways of the Lord. (Proverbs 3:6)

Accepting the assignment doesn't mean that it will be easy or even popular. Often it is just the opposite. You have to remember that for years we were afraid to simply leave our house. We were very lonely because we were not invited anywhere. There were the years that we never heard anything good being said about Hadley, only bad reports about what our child had done:

"Could you please keep your child quiet?" "Do you really think she belongs here?"

"She really caused a disruption for all of the others today!"

There was a period of time when we seemed to encounter trouble everywhere that we went.

Now, finally, by the grace of God and by applying the appropriate treatment, we were able to reveal the child that was meant to be.

Things were so different now. On more than one occasion while in elementary school, Hadley was invited to help brighten the attitude of teachers who might be having a rough day.

"Bring in Agent H," I was told the teacher would cry out. "Please, somebody, go get Hadley." Hadley would be brought into the lounge.

She would come in and just be her special self and all of the worries of the day would seem to drift away. Laughter, tender words, and sheer joy just seemed to envelope the distraught person when that child was near. It was as if people thought, with all of her issues, how could she be so unassuming, witty, cunning, and unpretentious? Surely I must be able to handle my own problems. Thank you, God, for using Hadley to show others how to cope. And the healing continued.

For years we questioned the move away from all that we were familiar with. A move away from all that we had worked so hard for. Not until three years later would we see how that move proved to be for our good. Now we understood that the move was part of the divine healing process not only for Hadley, but for us as well. God had repositioned us for our new assignment for his purpose. Now we were ready for the promotion. He knew what was best for us even when it didn't seem to make a bit of sense to us.

God continued to put people in our path that would be invaluable in terms of getting the help that we needed to begin the healing process for Hadley.

Make new friends but keep the old ……

And good old friends we had indeed, and we thank God for them. We had old friends that reached far back into my childhood. These were friends that were tried and true. These were the friends of my youth and had known me for most of my life. These were friends who knew us before, during and after the misfortunate diagnosis of autism.

These true-blue friendships began in my childhood and now their kids are my kid's friends. Because we have known them most of our lives, these friends are really more like relatives, the best kind of friends you can have.

These friends were a part of our deepest, most secret center of our lives. These friends participated in paramount events such as: babies first birthday parties, baptisms, family vacations, graduations, anniversaries, and even Grandma's sisters' second cousins' jewelry party. These esteemed friends, not surface acquaintances, were also privy to family confidential, cagey stories such as, "Heard cousin Betty stayed out pretty late with her boyfriend the other night, got in at two a.m." Or other juicy classic family gossip revealing such scoop as, "You do know that grandma was never really *legally* married to Grandpa?" Yes these were the treasured friends who had earned their right deep into the most inner core of our beings.

These were solid friends and these were the ones that

Hadley felt the most comfortable being around. No explanations were ever required, wonkiness and all, Hadley could just simply be her autistic self.

She could truly be accepted for her unique personality. And we didn't have to worry about what others' thought while with these friends, because these friends thought the world of Hadley. They loved every thing about her. And one particular miracle about these girls was that the season never ended, we never aged out.

Not only did they spend time with and help to fill the void for the long, lonely weekends of Hadley's past but also, they continue to this day to celebrate the seasons of Hadley's life.

The girls are Elaine, Jade, Alice and Alicia. I honestly believe that a life without them would have left Hadley empty.

The girls are genuine and their friendship allows opportunities for growth in areas of creativity, social peer relations, humor, but most importantly, a distinct look at what life may have been like without the diagnosis of autism. Hanging out with them is as if there were no autism at all, Hadley was just one of the girls. They're genuine relationship with Hadley proves she is just a normal kid, one of the gang.

One exceptional normal moment was the time that Elaine had won four tickets to a live studio audience on a popular T.V. cooking show called "Emeril Live." The show was filmed live in New York City and through a random contest she had been awarded four tickets. Elaine was thrilled with her good luck and choosing us to accompany her was an obvious resolution. Hadley was in the seventh grade at this time and though still low on academics was making great attempts socially.

Bill has always referred to himself as a self-proclaimed chef as he completes about ninety percent of the cooking in our home. I have to admit that over the years he has satisfied our palates with some rather succulent tasty dishes that could be fit for a king. So not surprising we loved watching The Food Network program as it appealed to our culinary interest and we watched it regularly. It was also the one time that Hadley would actually join us for a family activity. For some unknown reason she really enjoyed watching that particular program and would freely sit with us for its' hour duration. My hunch is that it was more of a show of action rather than one of dialogue that perhaps it somehow kept her attention and amused her. Emeril himself captivated her, as his mannerisms were so animated. And like her, he too had spontaneous outbursts with his speech as he would randomly yell out "BAM!" while crafting his culinary concoctions.

Hadley just loved that part of the show. She would laugh and laugh, It was almost as if she was mystically connecting with him, he was speaking her language.

"BAM, BAM!" whooped Emeril, while tossing generous handfuls of parsley on to his roast beef masterpiece.

"Bam, bam! This is how I finish this," he would boast.

"Bam, bam!" Hadley would laugh her head off mimicking and repeating as she watched Emeril.

"Ha, ha, ha, ha," Hadley would roar with laughter while

watching the weekly show in the family room with us. She seemed to really meld with this guy.

New York City, here we come. We were thrilled and yet, with an eleven year old autistic child in tow, we braced ourselves for the fear of the unknown, the unknown bizarre behavior that may unleash itself at any time and with out warning. So unlike a normal family, it was not unusual that we were experiencing enormous trepidation. What would it look like, our Hadley three thousand miles up in the sky, confined like packed sardines with complete strangers we wondered.

But surprisingly the airplane ride was a piece of cake. Lucky for us this particular flight had a pull down screen and movies were offered to the patrons on board. Hadley got to do her favorite thing in the world and that was watch movies to her hearts content. Submissively she sat pleased as punch. Eventually she even discovered the role of the generously, obliging flight attendants on board the aircraft and soon had them at her beckon call. Her impish grin and devious eyes winked at me as she accepted her second soft drink from the accommodating steward. There I sat two seats away, helpless, and unable to stop her impulsive indulgence. Hadley was flying the friendly skies and displayed absolutely no fears what so ever upon take off and descends as she lifted her hands way up high over her head, as if she were on some kind of roller coaster, and yelled out "WeeEEEEE," at the top of her lungs. Any hidden fears concealed by other passengers were soon put at ease as everyone around us cracked up in response to her entertaining behavior.

With a successful landing and no major issues on the plain, we headed for our limousine to transport us to the hotel.

This stretch of a ride provided plenty of legroom compared to the rather confining seats on the airplane. Hadley was having a field day in side of the enormous space of what seemed like a mobile playground. Her sensory stimulation was unleashed as she bounced from extra wide seat to seat. She had plenty of room to unwind and even move about within the playhouse on wheels. She rolled around on the thickly carpeted floor of the vehicle and under the bar that extended the entire length of the back portion of the vehicle. There was a table between the sofa like seats and a refrigerator off to the side by the interior doors. There was even a color TV protruding from the ceiling that Hadley managed to expertly tune into PBS network during our long limo ride through the congested traffic to the hotel—no problem.

Taking It To the Streets

There is something to be said about blending in with the crowd. And on crowded city streets we did find ourselves. There would be no worry about sticking out like sore thumbs in this over populated city. It was obvious that people seemed to be in an immense hurry and it was to our great advantage that no one seemed to make eye contact with any one. We wouldn't be seen. No one would notice that we were different. No one seemed to care. We wouldn't be judged. Hadley's jerking; gyrating, impulses and gait wouldn't be an issue here as she fit right in with some of the other quirky un noticed street people that we passed on the city side walks—all is good.

As for food, miraculously, gluten and dairy-free foods were offered on the menus of just about every restaurant that we had frequented—we were in heaven.

Let The Anxiety Begin

A day and a half later, upon successfully navigating the megalopolises with our Hadley we were finally sitting in the live studio audience getting ready to go live on the air in front of a million viewers. There were fast running camera crew wildly moving back and forth on the set; all the while the producer's assistant was coaching the audience.

"Through out the filming we are going to be holding up signs prompting you when it is time to applaud, laugh and make appropriate groans. No other sounds, I repeat, the sound tech instructed, no other sounds will be made."

"Yikes!" I gasped.

"The audience members will make no other sounds during any other time through out the show! Any questions?" she asked.

Yes, I have questions, I thought in my tormented mind, as I sat their frozen and questioning my sanity for ever thinking that we could pull this off.

"How do we get the heck out of here?" I asked rhetorically.

I gulped hard and try to keep myself from fainting.

Why didn't anyone warn them? Why didn't anyone tell them, these very important people, that there would be a very special child, an unusual child in their very important audience today?

Perhaps provisions of placing Hadley in to some sort of sound-proof booth could have been arranged, I thought wistfully.

Here we were trapped like rats in the middle of a very tiny studio audience with a million viewers. At home it appears to be ten times its size when watching from the comforts of your own living room.

Yes, we were trapped in very tight quarters with no way out. Being told to keep as still as possible, laugh only when told to do so, with an autistic child. Didn't they realize that that would be impossible?!

I could almost feel the walls closing in on us. I wanted to grab my Hadley and make a run for it. But there was no escape hatch. I could barely even remember how we got into the studio.

Then the voice returned, the voice that reminded me of who we were.

Who are you trying to kid? Who do you think you are? You are on live T.V. and you will ruin everything!

It was too late. I didn't have time to fight that old demon. I heard a loud buzz sound, saw the flash of a red light, heard a thud of closing doors and another loud voice say, "IN 3-2-1, YOU'RE ON!"

I don't know to this day if it was the fun, gentle face of Emeril welcoming us all to the T.V. audience that brought me back to life from my heart attack or what. But here we were, sitting in a live studio audience with Hadley and she seemed to be amused and content to sit still in her seat and watch Emeril, as he performed his culinary magic. It was all so surreal.

WE'RE GOING TO MAKE IT, I dared myself to believe it. Could Hadley actually sit through a live television show? A very popular one I might add. I fiercely hoped so. The audience was eerily quiet and still as Emeril prepared his masterful cuisine, and Hadley continued to sit still. I continued to pray without ceasing as I kept wiping huge drops of sweat from my brow.

This is normally a thirty-minute show if you are watching it by television at home. However, the live production is quite longer because we, the live audience, are still sitting right there in our seats during the commercial breaks for the viewers at home.

If you ever wonder what goes on during that time let me tell you that that is where all of the fun is.

The production crew steps in to high gear. They are ready to entertain us. They are much more relaxed while off of the air than on. They joke with the patrons and hand out goodies. They pat us on the back and tell us that we are the best audience ever. What people at home are not aware of is the staff, including Emeril stay right on the set with us. We couldn't believe it, there was Emeril himself, inches away from us, just hanging out.

All was going smooth and then he made his announcement: "COME ON DOWN!"

Emeril had just invited all of the kids in the audience to come on down to the center stage and have a treat with him.

How generous and sweet, I thought. *WHAAATT?!*

I was actually amazed at the number of kids that were in the studio audience that day. I was so focused and distracted with keeping my special child under my strong grip that I had forgotten that Emeril live was actually a family show and it wouldn't be unusual at all to see so many kids present. I was no more than thinking those thoughts as I watched those, well mannered, normal, fortunate kids marching down the aisle make there way to the stage when I recognized one that looked an awful lot like my Hadley.

HOLY COW! There was Hadley marching right in step, imitating to the best of her ability, with the rest of them. She wasn't doing too bad either, I thought.

I leaned over two seats to look at Bill. "Do something," I commanded.

He looked right back at me and just shrugged.

I looked at Elaine sitting right next to me.

"Let her go, she will be fine," she said.

At any rate it was too late, she was already down there along with all of the other kids laughing and talking with Emeril. Hadley was on the stage talking to Emeril!

For the record, this time when Hadley spoke, and we know that she did, we didn't know what she actually said, but when the words left her mouth Emeril was really cracking up. I guess we will never know.

We couldn't run there and grab her and make a commotion. But we were on the edge of our seats, on the "ready," ready for what ever might transpire next.

Emeril had opened up his fridge and offered all of the kids a Dove bar.

To my knowledge there are no such things as dairy-free dove bars.

There was my Hadley, as happy as a clam in a shell, looking back up at us. She knew that we were helpless, sitting ten rows back from the center stage. She knew that we were far enough away and would be too embarrassed to get up and make a scene. She is autistic, not stupid, and then she flashed that infamous impish grin and took her bite.

Cracking up, Elaine nudged me in the ribs and said "Isn't it great that we are the only three people in the studio who knew that Hadley is autistic?" she laughed.

I just nervously shrugged my shoulders as I kept an uncertain eye on my daughter.

FOOLED AGAIN!

"AND 3-2-1, YOU'RE ON..."

The girl friends were truly wonderful and notably affected Hadley's life.

Another time...

Even though these girls lived four hours away from us, they traveled the distance in order to help make Hadley's world a bit more normal. The time spent together was always filled with laughter and fun, so much so that I think that even Hadley forgot that she was autistic.

These girls loved to play board games and would tirelessly help to engage Hadley in order to participate. It was amazing to Bill and me how any other people, other than our selves, could get Hadley to play a game. These girls were able to accomplish that. Hadley would do her best with the help of some coaching to throw the dice and move around the board, guess at answers and simply play the game. But being who she was with her limitations and all from time to time she would have to get up and move around a bit, take a break, a lap or two just to re-group or refocus.

One time when Hadley took her stroll while we were playing cards the other kids and I didn't even notice Hadley's longer that usual absence.

"Jack, I just led, it is your turn," Alicia said. "Ok, Ok, I make it spades," replied Jack.

"You can make it spades all you want, cuz I am out!" Jade giggled as she slapped down her last card.

"But you didn't call last card," Jack scolded.

Suddenly, in the midst of all the finger pointing and table slamming and laughter, Hadley appeared. She seemed to be trying to tell us something but her lack of intelligent speech left her babbling. She was grunting and babbling something that sounded like, "Urb, urb."

We all just nodded our heads as if to acknowledge her as Jack continued to press on with his last card.

"Spades it is, follow or you are out," he commanded.

"Come and sit down Hadley," Alicia said gently. "The game is not over yet honey."

"Ther urb, ther burb," gibbered Hadley, taking another lap around the table and headed for the back porch instead of taking her seat.

"That's nice Hadley," Jack responded uninterested,

barely noticing the urgency in his little sisters' fragmented phrases.

"I wonder what Hadley is trying to tell us," Elaine queried. "She has come in here twice now."

"I think she wants to show us something on the back porch," offered Jade.

"Well, let's go and find out what it is," Jack finally said, as he realized that he was getting nowhere with the card game.

Just as everyone was throwing in their cards on to the center of the table Hadley came back into the room. This time she was running and laughing hysterically. She was laughing gasping and yelling, "Urb, urb!"

"Oh my gosh, duck!" instructed Jack as a big black bird the size of a crow came swooping over our heads.

Chairs were knocked over as we all tumbled and scrambled around the dinning room table trying to flee from the encroaching bird.

It was a scene of simultaneous ruckus. A wild rumpus of laughing and screaming filled the room as we weaved and bobbed and took at least three more laps around the dining table before heading towards the back porch.

"Open the door!" Alicia shouted.

"I got it," cried Jade.

Between Jack and the two girls swatting and screaming, they were finally able to shoo the intruding bird out through the door while the rest of us fled out into the backyard.

"That was cool," Jack laughed still trying to catch his breath.

"Look," Elaine shouted as she pointed up to the arbor in

the yard.

There hanging upside down on top of the arbor were Bill's shoes.

"It got Bill!" she cried.

We all broke out in fits of laughter.

Just then Bill was coming around the side of the house, barefooted with the garden hose in his hands, wondering what all the commotion was about. We tried to explain to a perplexed Bill that we were all playing cards and somehow Hadley let a black vulture-sized bird, into the house.

"Poor kid," Elaine explained to Bill. "She tried to tell us but we just ignored her."

"Yeah," Jack said. "She kept on saying 'Urb, urb.' She was obviously trying to tell us that there was a bird in the house."

"We need to pay more attention to that kid," I scolded.

"Yeah, just imagine if it had been a bear," Jack added.

Thank you Lord for hand picking the friends that have seeped into the isolated soul of Hadley and rescued her from her sequestered island.

A man of many companions may come to ruin,
But there is a friend who sticks closer than a brother.
Proverbs 18:24

God put the right friend in my path at the right time for me to obtain information regarding the integration of biomedical treatment. That applied information would begin to bring our child back to us. This alternative treatment approach taught me about the concept of the gluten-free, casein-free diet.

Through the research of this model, I learned that Hadley could not properly digest gluten and casein proteins that are found in foods containing wheat and dairy. I simply removed those food items from Hadley's diet, offering alternative food items instead. Not having much expectation or experience as to what would happen, after one week of substitution, I was quite amazed.

My mom and I were out in the backyard having lunch with Hadley. We were having our usual conversation about the spring flowers in our garden when Hadley suddenly interrupted, breaking her five-year silence.

"I am hungry," she announced. "I would love to have a hot dog!"

"That's nice, Hadley," I replied.

"*What?!*"

Well, I guess all of the struggles with the gluten-free diet finally paid off after all. Only one week on the diet and her speech came back, though we really had to be thick-skinned back in the early days. People thought that we were absolutely crazy when we explained that for medical reasons Hadley had to eat gluten-free, dairy-free foods. When we first moved to the small town, no one had heard of such an absurd concept or alien diet. Everyone I spoke with regarding this uncharted diet looked at me with skepticism and one eyebrow raised.

"Really, Mrs. Payne, you're starving that poor child to

death!" the fourth grade lunch aide scolded. "Just look at this lunch, it is pathetic!"

I tried to explain to people that this gluten free diet was not for fad, cosmetic or health crazed purposes. She simply could not digest the proteins found in gluten. Eating these foods would result in extreme tummy aches as well as put her into a mental fog.

Yes, it was quite pathetic in the early days of our gluten- free dairy free life. For one thing you couldn't find the GF/DF food products anywhere on earth much less in my small town. How do you feed your kid on this obscure diet when mainstream markets did not carry gluten or dairy-free items, period? There were no GF/DF imitations of our favorite foods anywhere to be found. No more bread, Twinkies, cakes, Doritos, Dairy Queen, pizza, or pop tarts. How would we survive?

If you did find such food items you had to be a really good sport to eat them. It was a difficult task to entice a little girl to eat breads and cookies that resembled bricks and mortar and Styrofoam and clay.

And these doleful food imposters were not cheep! You almost had to knock over a small bank to pay for them, as the price was exorbitant.

Gluten is a protein, the glue that binds or holds everything together, and it is found in just about every food on the planet. It's the binders, (gluten), that makes the food taste and feel really good. So it was no wonder (*wonder bread*) literally, that when Hadley would bite into her ham sandwich, with no gluten added in her bread, it would literally crumble apart and fall into pieces on her lunch tray. No wonder she would get frustrated and just push food aside, opting not to eat it at all.

In the beginning there was only one little health food store in our town at the time that could offer our special foods and they were sparsely stocked. We would have to wait weeks for simple breads or crackers to be delivered.

Now the word gluten-free is as common as the word Kleenex. You can find gluten-free products everywhere. All of the major supermarkets offer the precious GF/DF commodities of sustenance. And, oh, how the product has improved over the years.

Most major food brands have their own version of GF/DF cakes, cookies, pizza, and bread. Gluten-free foods have marched right into the main-street market making our culinary creations and palates much more satisfied.

Who'd of thought that fifteen years later the dreaded GF/DF foods would become trendy as they have?

Man does not eat by bread alone...

"I want a hot dog," Hadley continued.

Mom and I jumped up out of our chairs in shock that afternoon, screaming with delight at the sound of her beautiful voice. We couldn't believe our ears. Did Hadley just speak? Oh, God, it was a miracle! Had I really believed all those years ago that my daughter would never speak again?

And the healing continued.

In the beginning this diet was difficult to administer as far as food substitution, and it was imperative that she not deviate from its strict regiment. The other kids were trying their best to be supportive of her new dietary program but still wanted their own snacks. We decided to make a pact not to eat the foods in front of Hadley. If we were going to bring such foods into the house, we would do our best to conceal them. But Hadley with her sixth sense could sniff those snacks out like a hound dog. There were occasions where no matter how much physical pain might be involved; the temptation was just too great for a hungry little girl.

"Hadley, did you just eat all of my Doritos?" Lauren demanded.

"No," she said impishly as she wiped the cheesy snack from her lips.

"Mom, she is such a little food thief," her big sister teased. "Besides, I know that she is faking this autism thing. She is just pretending so that she doesn't have to do all the chores that Jack and I have to do."

I had to laugh in agreement with Lauren because sometimes Hadley was so intuitive and perceptive.

"Besides," Lauren continued, "she just smoked Jack and me again on the *Scene It* DVD game for the third time in a row."

Another time her brother Alan would go to his secret stash of his delicious Honey Buns only to find that all three left in the box had one bite out of each of them.

"Hadley!" he surmised.

"You know, Mom, if she had just gone ahead and eaten the whole thing, I never would have known. But no, she takes one bite out each one and leaves the rest there in the box. Like I'm not gonna know who did it!" he laughed.

As our focus changed from depending upon ourselves to depending on God, the sign of Hadley's healing was becoming crystal clear.

On Hadley's eighteenth birthday, Bill and I had to go to probate court in order to apply for guardianship of our daughter. We were all a bit nervous about this ordeal because well, as you know by now, one never knows what this precious child might say to people. For the past few months Hadley had been referring to Bill and me as the Kitty and the Dog. I think it may have been based on the movie *Cats and Dogs*, which had been released on DVD. We were almost through with this very formal meeting when the judge decided to ask Hadley a question.

"Well, Hadley, your parents are here today to obtain guardian rights for you. Do you have anything that you might want to say?"

"Why yes," she chirped. "My parents are a couple of animals."

The place fell apart with laughter. The judge tried his best to conceal his grin as he instructed the clerk to strike that from the record.

We thought for sure that this time someone would call the state workers. Lucky for us the judge was married to the school social worker. He was quite familiar with the "special kids" from the county. It was as if God had handpicked these people, this small town and community just for us. We had stumbled upon a great treasure.

Oh God, forgive me for doubting you. Thank you for the healing that you have bestowed upon us.

On this very special journey our family has been able to actively engage the autism culture. We accepted our call to live for Christ and His purpose for us. We hope to inspire people through the influence of our lives, to have a daily encounter with God, it is life changing.

"I need a hug in here," Hadley calls from the family room as she is watching *Lady and the Tramp*.

"I'll be right there with that hug, pumpkin," I answer, thinking back what seems like a million years ago now that she wouldn't let anyone touch her.

We continue to see improvement each day.

"Mom, I am going to take a shower after my show. Will you brush my hair? Please brush my hair?"

"I would love to brush your hair," I replied, remembering no more of those horrid battles of yesteryear.

Along the way we have also discovered by networking with other parents that, for some, autism can be reversible. We have also discovered that anything man puts his hand upon has room for error. Anything that God puts his hand upon has room for perfection. God truly wants to bless us. We are truly blessed.

"Daddy, I'm ready for you to tuck me in," Hadley called as she propped herself up between all of her furry friends on her bed.

"Which song tonight, baby girl?" Bill asked as he does each night.

"The lullaby song tonight, Daddy," she replied as she held her Lamb Chop doll.

> *Lullaby and good night.*
> *Close your sweet little brown eyes*
>
> *Lullaby and good night,*
> *You're the sweetest girl of all*
>
> *Lullaby and good night,*
> *You're an angel from God*
>
> *Lullaby and good night,*
> *Mom and dad love you so*

"Good night, Daddy."
"Good night, love-ish."

You have turned my mourning into joyful dancing.
Psalms 30:11

Afterword

Hadley was diagnosed with autism at the age of three. Hadley is now twenty-three years old upon the second edition of my story.

She is healthy, happy, and very social within the community. Hadley continues to attend school and reads and writes at about a sixth-grade level. With the aid of a job coach, Hadley holds three jobs in our community that include McDonald's, Holiday Inn, and Family Video. She successfully participated in Girl Scouts for thirteen years. She sings beautifully and was given a solo in sixth grade as well as in junior high. She sings weekly in our church choir and is very active in our youth group.

Hadley is an artist and expresses her world around her in a dramatic way through her drawings. Hadley is currently working on her own manuscript in order to tell her story to the world. She continues to teach us, as well as those that she encounters, to see the best in each person.

She loves and accepts everyone for who they are. She has an incredible sense of humor and can lift the darkest day with her infectious smile and amazing wit.

I don't know why afflictions and trials must occur on this side of heaven, but my journey to faith began in the midst of my crisis. It was there, in the middle of my ashes that I met a holy God who created us and cares deeply for us. I do believe that God hears our prayers and he even answers them, just not always in ways that we anticipate.

The Bible tells us if one little sparrow falls, the Father knows about it (Matthew 10:29). In the very beginning of our trials, I refused help from God or anyone else for that matter. I was very stubborn and unyielding while grappling with my dire circumstances. This selfish behavior actually held me back from helping my daughter when she needed me the most.

I write my story to inform others of the existence of autism and the desire for acceptance in society. It is also an informative tool to convey and possibly explore the options of alternative treatments that were available to us. Each child is unique on the autism spectrum, and what works for one may not work for another. And finally, and most importantly, it is a story about holding on to or rededicating one's faith in the midst of uncertainty. When we decided to put God back in to the center of our lives, everything began to change for the better.

"God is not unfair. He will not forget the work that you did or the love that you showed for Him in the help you gave to others" (Hebrews 6:10).

This collection of stories illustrates a few dismal

scenarios that actually seem funny now. Though dreadful at the time, a lesson was learned and we have found that people are generally good.

Those people appeared to be God himself, wrapped up in human clothing, showering us with help and genuine love. That kindness is like a soothing ointment, a salve bathed upon our souls.

Hadley truly is an agent "H." She is one of God's most effective ambassadors. She loves people unconditionally. She permeates goodness to all whom she encounters.

But the thing we love the most about her is that she prays so unabashedly and sincerely for others. Because of our faith and renewed relationship with God, we are able to devote the rest of our lives enriching our Hadley as she does the same for us.

I have a promise in Isaiah 41:13 that tells me that I am being up held by God's right hand and that I am not to be afraid for he will help me. He has given me a power that I didn't know that I had. He has given me the power to rise above the autism and make a difference not only for Hadley but for the lives of other's as well. God has taken my anger, depression and bitterness and replaced it with peace, hope and love. He has proven to be our only true hope. It is my desire that you have witnessed how our family was exposed to God's great blessings and provisions and that the same can hold true for you.

Give me happiness O Lord, for I give myself to you.

Psalms 86:4

MARY ANN PAYNE, M. A.

Bibliography

1. A Merriam-Webster, *Webster's New Ideal Dictionary*, 1973.

2. Gungor, Michael, "You Make Beautiful Things"

3. Baker, Sidney, M.D. and Pangborn, Jon, Ph.D: *Biomedical Assessment Options for Children with Autism and Related Problems, A Consensus Report of the Defeat Autism Now! (DAN!) Conference*, Dallas, Texas, January 1995. This version: April 1999, Introduction, PG 1.

4. Rimland Ph.D, Bernard, *Plain Talk About PDD and the Diagnosis of Autism*, Autism Research Review International, Vol. 7, No. 2, 1993, pg 3.

MARY ANN PAYNE, M. A.

Bill and Mary Ann before kids.

Six months old. Very normal.

Two years old. Despondent, not
wanting to play with others.

Three years old, starting to change.

Eight years old, wanting to participate, still not much speech. No longer making eye contact.

No interest in age-related activities.

Eight years old, wanting to participate, still not much speech. No longer making eye contact.

No interest in age-related activities.

Still no eye contact.

Attempting ballet lessons.

Easter morning, getting ready for church.

Hadley's first part in a church play.

The infamous beach toys.

Twelve years old. Jack trying to encourage Hadley to sing.

Fourteen years old. Hadley, a social butterfly, dressed-up for Halloween.

Hadley and Jan, her school aide.

Sixteen years old, singing
"Somewhere Over the Rainbow."

Seventeen years old. No longer afraid to sled.

Nineteen years old. High school senior picture.

High school graduation.

Twenty years old. Dressed and ready for work at McDonald's.

Hadley's Original Artwork

Hadley's perspective of herself, age 5, kindergarten.

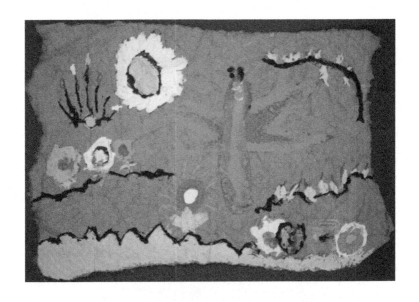

Hadley's new perspective of self, age sixteen.

Twenty four years old, displaying her latest work in a local art gallery.

Author contact information

Mary Ann has been going around the country telling her story. She delivers an inspirational message of divine hope regarding her journey. She loves and encourages any thoughts and feedback from her readers with reference to the "Hadley book." Please feel free to contact her at the following sites:

ma@bhe4me.com

www.facebook.com/hadley

Made in the USA
Middletown, DE
17 June 2023

32224828R00139